CW00746175

# The Council of Europe and human rights

An introduction to the European Convention on Human Rights

**Martyn Bond**

Council of Europe Publishing

French version:
*Le Conseil de l'Europe et les droits de l'homme – Une introduction à la Convention européenne des droits de l'homme*

ISBN 978-92-871-6901-3

*The opinions expressed in this work are the responsibility of the author and do not necessarily reflect the official policy of the Council of Europe.*

All rights reserved. No part of this publication may be translated, reproduced or transmitted, in any form or by any means, electronic (CD-Rom, Internet, etc.) or mechanical, including photocopying, recording or any information storage or retrieval system, without the prior permission in writing from the Public Information and Publishing Division, Directorate of Communication (F-67075 Strasbourg Cedex or publishing@coe.int).

The author acknowledges with thanks the assistance of Fiona Bywaters in the selection and preparation of cases referred to in this book.

Cover design: Les Explorateurs
Layout: Council of Europe Publishing
Photos: Council of Europe

Council of Europe Publishing
F-67075 Strasbourg Cedex
http://book.coe.int

ISBN 978-92-871-6836-8
© Council of Europe, June 2010
Printed at the Council of Europe

# Contents

# Human rights in Europe

## Human rights for our time

This little book offers a guide for the general reader to some of the key issues of human rights in Europe. If you are interested in knowing more about human rights – your rights – and how the Council of Europe protects and promotes them, read on. You will find a first section that lists the rights in the European Convention on Human Rights and its various protocols, then a section describing some of the cases that illuminate how these rights affect people in practice, a further section briefly describes how the European Court of Human Rights (the Court) functions, another describes how the Council of Europe tries in other ways to protect and promote human rights across the continent, and finally some comments on how human rights in Europe may expand and be strengthened in the near future.

In these pages you will find a simple description of what is a complex system. The Council of Europe is an umbrella organisation that brings together 47 states to promote democracy, human rights and the rule of law. It works by setting standards for the whole continent through conventions agreed – and then signed and ratified – by as many of the member states as possible. Being a central concern, the European Convention on Human Rights was the very first convention agreed by the states that set up the Council of Europe over 60 years ago, and it has been signed and ratified by all states that have since then joined the Council of Europe.

The European Convention for the Protection of Human Rights and Fundamental Freedoms – the full title of the European Convention on Human Rights or ECHR – was signed in 1950 and came into force in 1953. The ECHR did not come out of thin air. Like the Universal Declaration of Human Rights, promulgated by the United Nations in December 1948, it was the product of its time, the years immediately following the Second World War. The UN declaration was – and remains – a document of great moral value and authority, but it does not establish mechanisms for implementing the rights it proclaims. Only in the exceptional and specific circumstances of a war crimes tribunal does it create any procedure and set up a court to adjudicate on cases, to condemn the guilty and offer redress to victims. It does not put the member governments in the dock if they break the Universal Declaration's lofty aspirations. The ECHR went further and established the European Court of Human Rights, setting up legal mechanisms to enforce meaningful respect for human rights in Europe.

> The 10 initial signatories of the ECHR in 1950 were Belgium, Denmark, France, Ireland, Italy, Luxembourg, the Netherlands, Norway, Sweden and the United Kingdom. Since then all states joining the Council of Europe have signed and ratified the ECHR.

In the opening declaration of the ECHR the initial 10 states declared their resolution "as governments of European countries which are like-minded and have a common heritage of political traditions, ideals, freedom and the rule of law, to take the first steps for the collective enforcement of certain of the rights stated in the Universal Declaration".

## Never again!

It was the devastating experience of the Second World War that led European statesmen to strengthen the protection of the rights of individuals vis-à-vis the state. Arbitrary arrests, deportations and executions, imprisonment without charge, concentration camps and genocide, torture and show trials were part of very recent experience across much of Europe. European leaders wanted to protect future generations from such experiences. "Never again" was their watchword.

Western Europe learnt from its past mistakes and the Council of Europe, which was established in 1949, reflects a system of international relations based on the values of human rights, democracy and the rule of law – values clearly distinct from those underpinning either fascism or communism.

It not only lists civil and political rights for individuals; it also gives everyone in Europe practical protection for their rights by imposing obligations on states. The ECHR ensures the right of individual petition, which allows any individual to bring a case to the Court against his or her own state. It also provides for collective enforcement of the judgments of the Court of Human Rights, with states exposed to peer pressure and review by their colleagues in the Committee of Ministers, a body that sits in Strasbourg and reviews the Court's judgments to check that member states follow up what the Court decides.

Some of the most pressing political and ethical issues of our day relate to human rights. Whether the focus is on the treatment of those detained in the war against terror, on abortion or assisted suicide, on the freedom of the press or on the right to privacy, on gay marriage or on the restitution of property, all these issues involve human rights as laid down in the Convention. Although signed 60 years ago, it is now more than ever a document for our times.

The European Convention on Human Rights and the Court were created in the democratic states of western Europe in the 1950s, largely as a reaction to the recent flagrant abuses of human rights under fascism. They were later strengthened to contrast with the distortion of due legal process through one-party rule in the eastern half of Europe that was then under communist domination.

The ECHR acts as an example to other regions of the world. The Organisation of American States has established a court for the protection of human rights. The African Union has also adapted the European model.

Since then, growing numbers of people in Europe have enjoyed legal protection for a long list of rights and freedoms. They have at their disposal the European Court of Human Rights before which to demand redress if they think these rights have been abused. With the fall of the Berlin Wall in 1989, the collapse of communism across central and eastern Europe, and the break-up of the Soviet Union in 1991, many new states joined the Council of Europe. Now all 47 member states – from Iceland to

Armenia, from Portugal to Russia – accept the jurisdiction of the European Court of Human Rights in Strasbourg, and the Convention must be ratified by each state which joins the Council. All now subscribe to the protection and promotion of democracy, human rights and the rule of law, and in one form or another all 47 of them have built the ECHR into their national law. Their observation of it may be patchy and abuses of human rights certainly occur in Europe, but they can be brought before a court where the individual can seek redress against the state that has abused his or her rights. Nowhere else in the world can you do that.

## Rights and obligations

Many lawyers argue that human rights are "absolute" and have to be respected before all else. They also argue that they are "indivisible" and an abuse of one right weakens the protection of all rights. But human rights often have two aspects: a positive right which is often self-evident – the right to life and liberty, freedom of expression, of conscience and religion, the right to marry, for instance – and also a negative or balancing aspect, which may not be immediately apparent. Rights often conflict with each other, and rights often imply obligations.

Freedom of expression, for instance, implies limits that prevent one person's freedom of expression offending another, perhaps by intruding into their privacy. Hence the right implies an obligation to be tolerant. And even tolerance must know some limits, as excessive tolerance could lead to anarchy and the destruction of other human rights. The European Court's accumulated judgments, its case law or jurisprudence, offer a continuing commentary on just how far the rights enumerated in the ECHR should be asserted as "absolute" and how far their application in practice is balanced by other considerations. The circumstances of each case help to determine the nature and degree of respect accorded in practice to any right.

The ECHR is a dynamic document, interpreted by the Court in the light of the specific circumstances of each case. As Europe has developed over the past 60 years, rights have been added to the Convention by way of supplementary protocols – the right to education and to property, for example. And the Court's interpretation of the Convention has developed, lending now greater, now lesser emphasis to some of the balancing factors that inevitably qualify human rights in specific situations. In practice, the cases demonstrate and make the law.

## What rights are in the Convention?

The ECHR is a brief document, not even the length of this short book. The very first article ensures that the rights it lists apply to everyone "within the jurisdiction" of the states which sign up to it. Human rights are not restricted to citizens of the member states but apply to everyone living on their territory. States have a duty not to discriminate between individuals in that respect.

The rights themselves are listed in the first section of the ECHR, covering Articles 2 to 18, and some additional protocols.

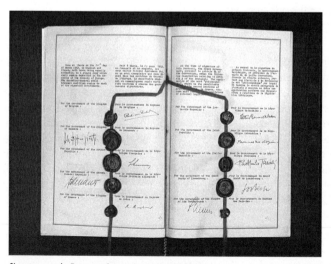

*Signatures on the European Convention on Human Rights.*

### Key rights in the ECHR

Right to life; prohibition of torture; prohibition of slavery and forced labour; right to liberty and security; right to a fair trial; no punishment without law; right to respect for private and family life; freedom of thought, conscience and religion; freedom of expression; freedom of assembly and association; right to marry; right to effective remedy; prohibition of discrimination.

Articles 2 to 18 cover the rights enumerated in the original Convention: the right to life, the prohibition of torture, of slavery and forced labour, the right to liberty and security, as well as the right to a fair trial and the prohibition of punishment without due process of law. The list goes on to include the right to respect for private and family life, freedom of thought, conscience and religion, freedom of expression, of assembly and association, the right to marry and the right – when these rights and freedoms are violated – to an effective remedy.

Subsequent amendments to the ECHR have added further rights. The first protocol (1952) added the protection of property, the right to education and the right to free elections. A later protocol (1963) concerned the prohibition of imprisonment for debt, freedom of movement, the prohibition of the expulsion of nationals from their state, and the collective expulsion of aliens. A protocol (1983) and another (2002) concerned the abolition of the death penalty. And another (1984) concerned safeguards relating to the expulsion of aliens, the right of appeal in criminal matters, compensation for wrongful conviction, the right not to be tried or punished twice for the same offence, and equality between spouses. Another protocol (2000) went beyond Article 14 of the ECHR, which refers only to non-discrimination in regard to the rights set out in the Convention, to introduce a general prohibition of discrimination in respect of any right set forth by law. Later pages of this brief guide will consider a selection of the rights enumerated in the ECHR and its various protocols, and relate them to cases that have come before the Court.

Over 20% of Court judgments find a violation of the right to a fair trial (Article 6) and over 25% relate to the excessive length of proceedings (also Article 6). A further 8% relate to abuse of the right to an effective remedy (Article 13).

The failure of states to protect the right to property (Article 1 of Protocol No.1) concerns a further 14% of judgments, while 10% relate to the right to liberty and security (Article 5), and about 8% of violations concern the right to life (Article 2) and the prohibition of torture or degrading treatment (Article 3).

## How relevant are Convention rights today?

Human rights, lawyers argue, hang together to form a closely knit set of rights and obligations, and chipping away at one part of them weakens them all. That is what they mean by rights being "indivisible". So states have to live up to high standards in a range of specific areas to show that they are not – unwillingly and perhaps unwittingly – starting off down a slippery slope towards a lack of respect for human rights as a whole. The onus is on public officials like the police and the military, the intelligence services, the judiciary and prison staff, on doctors and nurses, as well as on civil servants more generally and on politicians in government in particular, to observe high standards of behaviour as regards respect for human rights.

Cases considered in the pages which follow attempt to put flesh on the bones of this argument, but the general reader will already be aware of the issues surrounding "rendition flights" in Europe. Here some signatory states of the ECHR have admitted involvement in CIA flights intended to move terrorist suspects to detention centres where they could be subjected to torture – euphemistically called "enhanced interrogation techniques" – in order to obtain information that could help public authorities in the "war on terror". Such

### Rights added in later protocols

Right to property; right to education; right to free elections; prohibition of imprisonment for debt; freedom of movement; prohibition of expulsion of nationals; prohibition of collective expulsion of aliens; abolition of the death penalty; right of appeal in criminal matters; compensation for wrongful conviction; right not to be tried or punished twice; equality between spouses; general prohibition of discrimination.

actions, or complicity in such actions, raise serious questions about states' commitment to human rights, and the Court will doubtless be called on to pass judgment on different aspects of this when individual cases are brought before it.

The abuse of human rights is sometimes front page news, but at other times hardly publicised at all. Big issues may include the persecution of journalists and editors, discrimination against minorities, the denial of free elections or a ban on assembly and demonstration. But many cases relate to individual and highly personal issues, such as the continuation of slavery in a domestic setting, media intrusion into the privacy of family life, the restitution of property seized illegally in the political convulsions of recent European history or the right to a fair trial. The degree of media coverage is no measure of the importance of these issues to the individuals concerned. But the fact that the media frequently do cover cases before the Court is a measure of their awareness and concern for the seriousness of the issues to which the ECHR relates.

# Cases that make human rights law

Here we look at a selection of cases where the judgments of the European Court of Human Rights have interpreted the Convention in important and interesting ways. In this section of our guide we look at key rights, roughly following the order of the articles in the ECHR. Key elements of the text of various articles are highlighted on the relevant pages, so that readers have an easy point of reference.

While the ECHR itself is the fundamental point of reference, the Court's cumulative judgments – its jurisprudence or case law – guide the wider interpretation of human rights law throughout Europe. Inevitably this builds up slowly, and in a rather uneven pattern, as there are more cases relating to some of the articles than to others. But it steadily makes judges across the continent aware of judgments from Strasbourg, helps lawyers grasp the arguments deployed and see their relevance for cases they are dealing with nationally, and teaches students of law about the mechanisms of the Court and the importance of the ECHR. If national courts all delivered judgments that were in line with the provisions of the ECHR and the case law of the Court, then very few new cases would find their way to Strasbourg. Litigants would be satisfied that their human rights were adequately protected at home. Sadly, that is still far from the case.

So the Court has increasingly taken a proactive role in trying to speed up the understanding and application of case law in domestic courts throughout Europe. It organises seminars for judges and lawyers, encourages students of law to specialise in human rights, and publicises its judgments actively both in the media and on its own website. Together with the steady stream of judgments, these activities help guide the gradual emergence of common interpretations and common standards for the legal protection of human rights across the national jurisdictions of the continent.

The Court also offers "pilot judgments". Where there are a large number of applications concerning the same problem, applicants will obtain redress more speedily if an effective remedy is established at national level than if their cases are processed on an individual basis in Strasbourg. So the Court selects one or more from a large number of similar cases and renders a "pilot judgment", freezing the other cases for a period of time to allow the member state concerned to rectify the situation nationally. All this is in an effort to ensure that fewer cases come to Strasbourg and that the ECHR is better applied in the domestic or national courts of the member states.

# Human rights for everyone

### Article 1 – Obligation to respect human rights

The High Contracting Parties shall secure to everyone within their jurisdiction the rights and freedoms defined in Section 1 of this Convention.

All states which are members of the Council of Europe have a legal duty to respect human rights and to ensure that they apply to everyone in their jurisdiction. States cannot be selective, preferring one group of citizens – for instance, their own nationals – to another, as human rights are universally applicable. And they have an obligation to ensure that the rights of the ECHR are applied throughout their territory, not allowing areas of lawlessness in which human rights can be ignored or abused. This issue came to the fore in a recent case from Georgia where a convicted person was not released from jail in an autonomous region of the country after his pardon and the order for his release had been issued by the central authorities.

> Tengiz Assanidze was sentenced to eight years' imprisonment in 1994 for illegal financial dealings and possession of firearms and was committed to prison in the Ajarian Autonomous Republic. Five years later he was pardoned by the President of Georgia, but was not released by the Ajarian authorities. While he was still being held, but after his pardon, he was tried locally on an additional charge of kidnapping and was sentenced by the Ajarian High Court to a further 12 years in prison. He was subsequently acquitted by the High Court of Georgia which ordered his release in 2001. More than three years later he was still in custody in a prison run by the Ajarian Security Ministry.

The Court judgment recognised that the central authorities in Georgia had done all that they could under domestic law to secure compliance with the judgment acquitting the applicant. They had tried to resolve the issue by political means and had repeatedly urged the Ajarian authorities to release him, but all to no avail. Nonetheless, it was the responsibility of the Georgian state to find a solution to the problem. As a signatory of the ECHR, Georgia undertook to secure the rights and freedoms of the Convention for everyone within its jurisdiction, without exception or reservation. That is what Article 1 of the ECHR implies (*Assanidze v. Georgia, 2004*).

## Life and death

Europe is the only continent where the death penalty has been abolished. Or, to be more exact, it has been abolished in almost all of Europe. Let's look at how we got to where we are.

The experience of arbitrary killing in wartime was still strong in the minds of those who drafted the ECHR in 1950. But public opinion at the time that the Convention was originally adopted was not clearly in favour of abolition of the death penalty for serious crimes such as murder. In negotiating Article 2 of the ECHR (protecting the "right to life") governments only went so far as to limit the use of force by the state to cases where it was provided for by law or was necessary to oppose force, for instance defending someone from unlawful violence, effecting a lawful arrest or preventing a prisoner's escape, or when quelling a riot or insurrection. Capital punishment was not then in question.

Back in the 1960s, the Parliamentary Assembly of the Council of Europe, less constrained by responsibilities of government, began a debate on the subject of the death sentence with the aim of making Europe the first region in the world to permanently eliminate capital punishment. This culminated in the adoption of Protocol No. 6 which came into force in 1985. This prohibits recourse to the death penalty except in time of war. Now the Council of Europe requires new states that wish to join at least to implement a moratorium on capital punishment and to commit to ratifying Protocol No. 6 of the ECHR.

But Protocol No. 6 was not the final step in the Council of Europe's efforts towards eliminating the death penalty throughout the continent. Protocol No. 13, which abolishes the death penalty under all circumstances without any derogation or reservation, was agreed in 2002. Not all states, however, are yet prepared to go that far. This protocol entered into force in July 2003 but, unlike Protocol No. 6, it has not yet been ratified by all member states and is not yet an obligation of Council of Europe membership.

Russia has signed Protocol No. 6 but has never ratified it, although the Russian Constitutional Court concluded late in 2009 that imposing the death penalty or carrying out the death sentence would be illegal in Russia in view of its international commitments. Ratification of the protocol may soon follow.

As for Protocol No. 13, 42 of the 47 states of the Council of Europe have signed and ratified it. Three – Armenia, Latvia and Poland – have signed but not yet ratified, and two others – Russia and Azerbaijan – have not yet signed.

The last execution in Armenia was carried out nearly 20 years ago, and the country signed Protocol No. 13 in 2006. In Spain, a law of 1995 abolished the death penalty in all circumstances, but the constitution permits its re-establishment by military penal law in time of war. Despite adopting a new penal code in 1998 which abolished the death penalty for all crimes, Poland has still not ratified Protocol No. 13. The Latvian Criminal Code, as amended in 2000, prohibits the death penalty for women and individuals under the age of 18, and the Latvian Parliament considered the question of ratifying Protocol No. 13 in 2002. As yet, however, Latvia has not taken this step.

The Council of Europe Commissioner for Human Rights, Thomas Hammarberg, has described the death penalty as a "fallacious idea of justice" and has criticised its apparent legitimisation of extreme violence by the state. His criticisms stress the ineffectiveness of capital punishment in deterring crime, the risk of executing an innocent person and the tendency of its implementation not to be uniform, with the victims of executions being more often poor people and from ethnic minorities.

In Belarus, often described as "the last dictatorship in Europe" and not yet a member of the Council of Europe, the constitution permits capital punishment for "grave crimes" against the state or against individuals, even those of a non-violent nature. Since 1994, the death penalty has exceptionally no longer been allowed against women, those under 18 at the time of the crime, or those over 65 at the time of sentencing. But as recently as October 2009, the Belarus Supreme Court once again rejected an appeal against the death penalty and an execution was still pending at the time.

Around the world, the ethics of capital punishment continue to be hotly debated. China, the most prolific in handing out death sentences, has recently pledged to reduce the number of people it executes. Kyrgyzstan, however, is considering a return to the death penalty in response to an increasing murder rate, and there are suggestions there that executions may be held in public. Japan and the United States – both enjoying observer status at the Council of Europe – still retain the death penalty. According to Amnesty International, prisoners on death row in Japan may be driven to insanity by harsh conditions including many years in isolation. In the United States, the Supreme Court delivered as recently as 1976 a judgment that declared the death penalty constitutional, and only 15 states have abolished it.

## The right to life

There is no more fundamental right than the right to life. If that is not respected, little else matters. Hence the ECHR and the casework of the European Court of Human Rights accord this right the highest importance. Over the years, the Court has dealt with cases that involve both the active agency of states in depriving people of that right and their failure to act, which has caused loss of life.

Sometimes such cases attract considerable media attention, especially when they lift the curtain on state involvement around issues of security. Sometimes they pass almost unnoticed by the wider world, exposing little more than administrative negligence or slack execution of standard procedures by prison staff, police or other agents of state authority.

## Death by police negligence

Such appeared to be a case of domestic violence, for instance, in Slovakia in 2007.

> A widow claimed that failures by the police to take seriously a case of domestic violence led to the murder of her children by her husband and his subsequent suicide. Given a history of domestic violence within the family, with one incident previously involving a firearm, the police should have followed correct procedures in registering the wife's complaint, launching an investigation, starting criminal proceedings against the husband, keeping a proper record of emergency calls and informing local police officers of the situation as they came on duty.

The domestic courts in Slovakia themselves subsequently established that the police failed to ensure these obligations were complied with, and that as a direct consequence, the applicant's children were killed by her husband. The Slovakian Government also acknowledged before the Court that the domestic authorities had failed to take appropriate action to protect the children's lives. The Court was unanimous in declaring a violation of Article 2, the right to life (*Kontrova v. Slovakia, 2007*).

## Killing on suspicion

In March 1988, at the height of the "Troubles" in Northern Ireland, there was a much more dramatic incident that received extensive media attention. It was brought to the Court by the families of three IRA terrorists shot dead in Gibraltar by undercover members of the UK Special Air Service (SAS).

> The British authorities knew that the suspects were planning a bomb attack, and had the suspects under surveillance. Thinking the three suspects were about to detonate remote control devices, the soldiers opened fire. But no weapons, bombs or detonators were found on the bodies or in the suspects' car.

Considering the case against the United Kingdom, the Court observed that the "use of force" mentioned in paragraph 2 of Article 2 of the Convention must be no more than "absolutely necessary" for the achievement of one of the purposes of that paragraph – defence from unlawful violence, lawful arrest, preventing escape, quelling riot or insurrection. And it accepted that the soldiers themselves believed it was necessary to shoot the suspects in order to prevent them detonating a bomb and killing innocent people. The use of force by agents of the state could be justified where it is based on an honest belief, perceived to be valid at the time but which subsequently turned out to be mistaken. So the Court held that the reaction of the soldiers did not, in itself, give rise to a violation of Article 2.

But the Court also took a broader view, considering the decision of the British authorities not to prevent the suspects from travelling to Gibraltar in the first place, their failure to allow for the possibility that intelligence assessments might be erroneous, and the recourse to lethal force immediately when the soldiers opened fire. On this basis, the Court concluded in a very carefully worded judgment that it was not persuaded the killing of the three terrorists constituted a use of force which was "no more than absolutely necessary in defence of persons from unlawful violence within the meaning of Article 2, paragraph 2 of the European Convention". So, in effect, these killings did constitute a violation of Article 2 of the ECHR (*McCann and others v. the United Kingdom, 1995*).

## Disproportionate force

Excessive use of force by the police is often the trigger for cases regarding the right to life which come to the Court in Strasbourg, and that was so in a case concerning Bulgaria in 2005.

> Two Roma conscripts were shot dead by military policemen in Bulgaria who had been ordered to arrest them on a minor charge. The regulations on the use of firearms by the military police effectively permitted them to use lethal force when arresting soldiers even for the most minor offences.

Such a legal framework was fundamentally deficient, falling far short of the level of protection of life required "by law" under the Convention, said the Court. In addition, in this case the military police had been instructed to use "all available means" to arrest the soldiers, despite the fact that they were unarmed and posed no danger. The manner in which the operation was planned and controlled betrayed a "deplorable disregard for the pre-eminence of the right to life".

The subsequent failure of the authorities to mount an effective and thorough investigation of the incident compounded the offence. The investigating authorities ignored significant facts without seeking any proper explanation, accepting instead the military police version of events. The Bulgarian authorities' conduct in such investigations – remarked on in previous cases by the Court – was a matter of grave concern, casting doubt on the impartiality and objectivity of the investigators and prosecutors concerned. Not surprisingly in these circumstances, the Court found that Bulgaria had violated Article 2 both in the killing of the conscripts, and also in failing to meet its obligation to investigate the case effectively (*Nachova and others v. Bulgaria, 2005*).

## Death in police custody

In October 2007 the Court also condemned France for a violation of Article 2 in a case concerning the arrest of Mohammed Saoud.

> Saoud, a young schizophrenic, seriously injured some of the police officers sent to arrest him for a minor offence. The rough treatment he received at the hands of the police during the early stage of his arrest was considered by the Court to be proportionate to the violence of his conduct. However, the Court accepted that subsequently holding him face down on the ground for 35 minutes with arms and legs immobilised had led to slow asphyxia, cardiac failure and death, and this treatment clearly contravened the victim's right to life.

The Court deplored the fact that no precise instructions had been issued by the French authorities with regard to this type of immobilisation technique. Despite the presence at the scene of professionals trained in emergency assistance, no treatment was given to the young man. Accordingly, the Court judged that the authorities had failed in their obligation to protect the life of Mohammed Saoud, and there had been a violation of Article 2 (*Saoud v. France, 2007*).

## A right to die?

It would be wrong to give the impression that the Court always finds a violation of a basic right in cases brought before it. On occasion the Court finds no violation, and these cases can raise interesting points of law. They test the boundaries of what is or is not acceptable in contemporary society, such as the conditions in which life begins and ends, from conception to death. Judgments frequently touch on sensitive areas of social concern, often ruffling religious convictions, for instance cases relating to stem cell research, IVF and abortion, or issues surrounding euthanasia.

> Take, for instance, the recent case brought by Diane Pretty, a British woman with advanced motor neurone disease. She argued that a refusal by the national authorities to give an undertaking in advance not to prosecute her husband for assisting her to commit suicide breached her right to life under Article 2 of the ECHR.

In its case law in this area the Court has placed consistent emphasis on the obligation of states to protect life. In the circumstances of this case it was not persuaded that the "right to life" guaranteed in Article 2 could be interpreted – without distortion of language – as conferring an opposite "right to die". Nor could it create a right to self-determination in the sense of giving an individual the right to choose death rather than life.

So here the Court accordingly found that no right to die, whether at the hands of a third person or with the assistance of a public authority, could be derived from Article 2. There had therefore been no violation of that provision in this case. But subsequently, in the light of the heated public debate that the case gave rise to in the UK, the authorities there clarified the law, issuing detailed instructions concerning the circumstances in which the Director of Public Prosecutions would or would not bring charges against anyone assisting a relative to die (*Pretty v. the United Kingdom, 2002*).

## Torture, inhuman and degrading treatment

For many years Europeans, especially those living in the democratic half of Europe before the collapse of communism, assumed that torture was a thing of the past, banished to the oubliettes of distant history. Torture chambers were exhibits in museums, seen as tourist attractions, not as instruments of contemporary state control or coercion. But a penetrating report by Swiss Senator Dick Marty for the Council of Europe's Parliamentary Assembly in 2008 revealed that, much more recently, several European

> **Article 3 –**
> **Prohibition of torture**
>
> No one shall be subjected to torture or to inhuman or degrading treatment or punishment.

states have collaborated with the USA in the "war on terror" by condoning torture. Complicity in CIA "rendition flights", moving terrorist suspects across Europe to detention centres where they risked being exposed to "enhanced interrogation techniques", has been acknowledged by several states. As Guantanamo Bay detention centre is run down and prisoners sent to different countries in Europe, cases may yet work their way through the national courts to reach the European Court of Human Rights. It is a chapter still open in the ongoing story of the protection of human rights in Europe.

It is not just the contemporary aspect of the treatment of suspected terrorists that preoccupies the Court. Over the years it has established jurisprudence through a range of other cases, spotlighting areas of concern where states have abused the right of individuals not to be subjected to such treatment. They range from physical abuse of political opponents to corporal punishment for juvenile delinquents, from the forcible administration of emetics to the rigours of military service, and they even reach as far as extradition to countries where applicants may face the death penalty.

## Torture of opposition leader

In most states we are used to the peaceful handover of political power in the wake of free and fair elections, but that is not necessarily true over the whole of the continent. Recently a case against Azerbaijan threw a light on less tolerant practices as regards political opposition.

> Sadar Jalaloglu was Secretary General of the Democratic Party of Azerbaijan, one of the opposition parties that considered the presidential elections of October 2003 to be illegitimate. He was arrested after a political demonstration against the result of the elections, charged with "organising public disorder" and "use of violence against state officials" and prevented from seeing his lawyer for several days. He was sentenced to three years in prison, but was subsequently released early by presidential pardon.

torture

He complained to the European Court of Human Rights that he was ill-treated during police custody, notably being beaten on the soles of his feet (*falaka*) by two masked policemen, and threatened with rape. This violated Article 3 of the ECHR, the prohibition of torture.

The Council of Europe's Committee for the Prevention of Torture had previously confirmed that *falaka* was one of the forms of ill-treatment used in Azerbaijani detention centres, and given the circumstances of this case, the Court considered the nature of the injuries Sadar Jalaloglu had suffered were attributable to torture for which the authorities were responsible, and that they had violated Article 3 (*Mammadov [Jalaloglu] v. Azerbaijan, 2007*).

## Flogging or slippering: inhuman or just degrading?

The casework of the Court has consistently distinguished between three degrees or aspects of treatment or punishment mentioned in Article 3 – "torture" as the most severe, "inhuman" as the next most severe, and "degrading", the least severe level of abuse. Two cases, both regarding the United Kingdom, bring out some of these distinctions.

> Before 1978 the official punishment for assault on the Isle of Man – a part of the United Kingdom which enjoys considerable self-rule – was three strokes of the birch, administered on bare buttocks. In a case decided by the Court that year, it was established that, while clearly not "torture", flogging or birching as a punishment did nonetheless violate Article 3.

The Court declared that, for a punishment to be degrading, the "humiliation or debasement involved must attain a particular level and must in any event be other than the usual element of humiliation" associated with conviction. The fact that the article expressly prohibits "inhuman" and "degrading" punishment clearly distinguishes this from punishment in general. So the humiliation of conviction by a court itself is not an issue, but the nature or manner of the punishment imposed may be.

This assessment, the Court conceded, must necessarily be relative, depending on the circumstances of the case and in particular "on the nature and context of the punishment itself and the manner and method of its execution". However, it was not classified as "inhuman" punishment, as the Court concluded the suffering occasioned must attain a particular level of intensity before a punishment can be classified as "inhuman". In this case, in the Court's view, it did not (*Tyrer v. the United Kingdom, 1978*).

> Corporal punishment consisting of three whacks with a rubber-soled gym shoe on the bottom of a 7-year-old boy by the headmaster of a private school, however, was not severe enough even to constitute "degrading treatment". The Court noted that the boy had been at school only five weeks and the punishment was administered three days after he was told he would be corporally punished, causing him several days' apprehension. Even so, the circumstances were not sufficient to justify a judgment indicating a violation of Article 3.

Four judges entered a dissenting minority opinion in this case, on the grounds that the ritualised character of the corporal punishment – notably the three-day delay before being inflicted – was cause enough for this to constitute degrading punishment, and hence a violation of Article 3, but the majority judgment stood (*Costello-Roberts v. the United Kingdom, 1993*).

## Over-zealous police action

When German police picked up a small-time drug dealer, they did not realise how far his case would go.

> Abu Jalloh originated from Sierra Leone and in 1993 he was living in Cologne, selling small packets of cocaine which he secreted in plastic bags in his mouth. He spoke no German and only broken English. As the police arrested him, he swallowed the last remaining bag, and it was what the authorities did then that caused the trouble. Since the police found no other drugs on him, the public prosecutor ordered that he be given an emetic in order to regurgitate the swallowed bag. When he refused to take medication to induce vomiting, four police officers held him down while the medication was inserted through a tube in his nose, and he was also given an injection to ensure it worked. On the basis of the regurgitated packet of drugs he was subsequently convicted and sentenced.

The Court reiterated that the Convention did not, in principle, prohibit recourse to forcible medical intervention to assist the investigation of an offence. But in this case the Court was not satisfied that the forcible administration of emetics was indispensable to obtain the evidence. The prosecuting authorities could simply have waited – as is the practice in several other countries – for the drugs to pass out of the applicant's digestive system naturally.

The Court also noted that there was no agreement on the danger of administering emetics. It had previously caused two deaths in Germany and authorities in most Council of Europe states refrained from applying this method. The Court found that the German authorities had subjected the applicant to a grave interference with his physical and mental integrity against his will. Although it had not been their intention, the manner in which the authorities implemented the measure had caused him both physical pain and mental suffering. Hence he had been subjected to inhuman and degrading treatment contrary to Article 3 (*Jalloh v. Germany, 2006*).

## Military call up for septuagenarians?

Some cases, you might think, merit the Guinness World Records rather than the time of the Court. But to the applicants they are an integral part of their experience and the suffering can be something they take with them to their grave.

> Take the case of Hamdi Tastan, an illiterate Kurdish shepherd, who lived far from any city, working in exchange for food and shelter on a subsistence basis in an obscure village in Anatolia. It was not until 1986, quite late in his life, that he was registered in the Turkish civil status register. All was well until a quarrel in 2000 in his home village led to him being falsely denounced by neighbours as a deserter. He was arrested by local gendarmes and taken to a military recruitment office where he was required to do military service. Despite being 71 years old, he was certified medically fit and transferred to a training centre. There he was forced to take part for a month in the same activities and physical exercises as 20-year-old recruits. Hamdi Tastan claimed he was subjected to degrading treatment during his training, forced to pose with superiors for photos and made the target of jokes. He also had difficulty eating army rations as he had no teeth. After training he was transferred to an infantry brigade where his state of health

deteriorated, and he was later admitted to a military hospital. Two months after his "recruitment" he obtained a certificate exempting him from military service on grounds of heart failure and old age.

The Court declared that a state had to provide a plausible explanation for the cause of any harm to the physical or mental integrity of persons placed under its control. In Hamdi Tastan's case that requirement had not been satisfied. The applicant's military service records had been destroyed by the authorities, but it was not contested that he had been hospitalised after participating in training alongside recruits 50 years younger than himself. Nor had they specified whether there had been any public interest in forcing him to perform military service at such an advanced age. In summary, the Court found that this amounted to degrading treatment within the meaning of Article 3 of the ECHR (*Tastan v. Turkey, 2008*).

## Is being on death row inhuman punishment?

In 1989 the Court gave judgment in a case where Article 2 (Right to life) and Article 3 (Prohibition of inhuman or degrading treatment) raised the issue of respect for human rights in states outside the Council of Europe.

It arose in an appeal by Jens Soering, a German national who committed a double murder in the United States and fled to the United Kingdom to avoid prosecution. The United States requested his extradition in 1986 and by summer 1988, when all UK legal processes had been exhausted, he appealed to Strasbourg.

The Court confirmed that the extraditing state – in this case the UK – could be held responsible for a breach of the Convention where it was aware of a real risk that the person concerned might be subject to inhuman or degrading treatment if they were extradited. The fact that he or she might be subjected to the death penalty was not, however, the reason to prevent extradition, as that penalty, as such, was not prohibited absolutely by the Convention. Other factors, such as the manner by which the death penalty was administered, the personal circumstances of the detainee, and the sentence's lack of proportion with the gravity of the crime committed, as well as the conditions of detention, could all, however, violate Article 3.

In the case of Soering, it concluded that the "death row phenomenon" did breach Article 3, because of the likely length of detention prior to execution, the conditions of detention on death row and the applicant's age and mental condition. The Court also noted the possibility that he might have been extradited to Germany – instead of the United States – where he would not have been subjected to a comparable abuse of his human rights, since he would still have been subject to the ECHR and the jurisdiction of the Court there (*Soering v. the United Kingdom, 1989*).

This case considerably enlarges a state's responsibility for breaches of the Convention. Even if assurances of fair treatment are given by another state and the actual treatment in that third country is beyond the extraditing state's control, the signatory state has to consider these consequences as being part of its responsibility. It means that the responsibility of signatory states is implicitly extended to acts carried out in non-signatory states, and the ECHR is presumed to override agreements concluded with such states. The rationale of the Court's judgment applies equally to deportation as well as extradition cases, where other articles of the Convention covering other rights may be at stake, for instance Article 6 (Right to a fair trial).

# Liberty and security

Given that the ECHR was drawn up shortly after the end of the Second World War, it is hardly surprising that those drafting it ensured there was an article prohibiting slavery and forced labour. Forced labour had been widely used by the Nazis, conscripting skilled and unskilled workers in the countries they occupied and forcing them to work for the German war effort. And even today, in more private settings, exploitation can amount to slavery.

**Article 4 – Prohibition of slavery and forced labour**

No one shall be held in slavery or servitude.

No one shall be required to perform forced or compulsory labour.

In democratic societies subject to the rule of law we are all free in the most general of senses, and given a wide range of personal choices within the range of our economic possibilities, our cultural customs, our social expectations and the law of the land. That gives us relatively wide freedom to act and relatively few constraints on that freedom. The resulting variety of lifestyles makes up much of the richness of European society. But for some people there are many more constraints which limit their freedom, especially for those with restricted economic means and little or no social and family network of reference and support.

The full text of this article does permit compulsory labour in certain circumstances, for instance as part of a prison sentence, or as military service or recognised service as a conscientious objector, or in response to a national emergency, or as part of normal civic obligations. But it expressly prohibits slavery and forced labour outside these circumstances.

The issue of constraints and, in the most extreme cases, of slavery has come to the fore with the growth of immigration into Europe in recent years. Migrant workers exploited by unscrupulous employers and "gang-masters", or women and children trafficked into Europe for sexual exploitation, give a new human face to an old phenomenon.

## Domestic slavery

In 2001 the Parliamentary Assembly of the Council of Europe regretted that "none of the Council of Europe member states expressly made domestic slavery an offence in their criminal codes". And as recently as 2005 France was condemned by the Court for the inadequacy of its law on "domestic slavery".

> The case in point concerned a Togolese girl brought to Paris illegally and forced to work seven days a week for four years from early morning to late at night as an unpaid "maid of all work" for a family with small children. Her "employers" kept her passport, and without legal residence papers she was initially afraid to complain about her situation.

When the case reached Strasbourg, the Court stated that Article 4 enshrined one of the fundamental values of the democratic societies which make up the Council of Europe. The prohibition of slavery, servitude and forced labour was a provision where it was not enough for states simply to refrain from infringing the guaranteed rights. They had a positive obligation to adopt and implement effective provisions making this abuse a criminal offence.

Given the continuing prevalence of "domestic slavery" even in modern Europe, the Court considered that states were under an obligation to penalise and punish any act aimed at maintaining a person in a situation incompatible with Article 4.

The ECHR places a positive obligation on states to put right legislation which is inadequate or contrary to human rights, so that the Court is not faced with a stream of repeated cases to be judged as violations of the Convention. It is not enough to declare human rights in the Convention, even if individuals then have the right to bring cases against their own governments. The point is to change the law – or the application of the law – so that repeated cases do not come before the Court in Strasbourg (*Siliadin v. France, 2005*).

## Right to personal security

Liberty in a more classic sense implies not liberty to choose a way of life but liberty from interference by the state, in particular from arbitrary detention. This is the form of liberty that secures and preserves personal security.

> After their arrest at a demonstration against arms sales, five plaintiffs were condemned by courts in the United Kingdom. The first two refused to be bound over to keep the peace and were committed to prison for 28 days and seven days respectively. The other three were arrested at the demonstration while distributing leaflets and were detained by police for no more than a few hours. All five appealed to the Court, complaining that their arrest and detention had not been "prescribed by law" as required under Article 5, paragraph 1.

In summary, the Court found that in the first two cases the refusal of the two individuals to be bound over to keep the peace warranted their detention, since they would give no assurances that they would not intensify or escalate their protests. Hence the Court found that no violation of their right to liberty and security had occurred.

But in the case of the three other protestors, they were not causing, nor were likely to cause, a breach of the peace – defined as causing harm, or being likely to cause harm, to persons or property or acting in a manner likely to provoke

### Article 5, paragraph 1 – Right to liberty and security

Everyone has the right to liberty and security of person. No one shall be deprived of his liberty […] in accordance with a procedure prescribed by law.

others to violence. The three protestors had acted entirely peacefully, not giving the police any cause to fear a breach of the peace.

Hence the Court found that their arrest and detention – even for a few hours – had not been lawful and was disproportionate, constituting a violation of Article 5. In addition it had infringed their right to free expression as contained in Article 10, where there had also been a violation of the ECHR (*Steel and others v. the United Kingdom, 1998*).

## Detained to contain infection

A homosexual with HIV appealed against repeated court orders in Sweden keeping him in compulsory isolation in hospital. This measure was taken to prevent the further spread of HIV through sexual contact. The court orders – for six months at a time – were issued from 1995 to 2001, but the applicant frequently absconded, so that the total time spent in isolation (actually deprived of liberty) was not more than 18 months.

The Court had to decide whether this deprivation of liberty amounted to "the lawful detention of a person in order to prevent the spreading of infectious diseases" as stated in one of the sub-clauses of Article 5, paragraph 1, of the Convention. It found that there were two key criteria: whether the spreading of the infectious disease was dangerous for public health or safety, and whether detaining the person was the last resort in order to stop the spreading of the disease. Could less severe measures have been considered or applied?

While HIV was certainly dangerous for public health, the Court was not persuaded that less severe measures than compulsory isolation would not have been sufficient to counter the threat of spreading the disease. There was no evidence that the applicant had spread the infection to other people during times when he was away from isolation, nor that he had had sexual intercourse without informing his partner of his infection, or using a condom, or indeed that he had had sexual intercourse at all.

The Court ruled that the authorities had failed to strike a fair balance between the need to ensure that the HIV virus did not spread and the applicant's right to liberty, and that compulsory isolation in hospital in this case did constitute a violation of Article 5 of the Convention (*Enhorn v. Sweden, 2005*).

# A fair trial

Once the right to life and freedom from torture, inhuman or degrading treatment are assured and you are not deprived of your liberty, what matters most – if you are nonetheless arrested – is that you receive a fair trial. The ECHR ensures this through Articles 6 and 7, concerning respectively the right to a fair trial and the right not to be punished if there is no law. In a later protocol, No. 7 agreed in 1984, it further spells out rights regarding the right of appeal in criminal matters, compensation for wrongful conviction and the right not to be tried or punished twice for the same offence.

More than one case in five where the Court finds a violation of the ECHR concerns the right to a fair trial. The reasons given for such judgments range from unreasonable delays in pre-trial detention, partial judges, manifest failure to presume the accused to be innocent until proved guilty, and certain procedural deficiencies, such as a lack of access to witnesses or inadequate time for the preparation of a defence. On occasion the issue turns on the right of the accused not to incriminate themselves, sometimes through evidence obtained under duress.

## Confession under torture

Such a case was brought by an Armenian, Mr Harutyunyan in 2007, who claimed that his conviction for murder in 1999 was obtained by relying on a self-incriminating confession obtained through torture. Referring to Article 6, paragraph 1 of the Convention, he complained that his right not to incriminate himself and his right to a fair trial had been breached by the use at his trial of statements which had been obtained from him and from two witnesses through torture.

The Court noted that the fact the applicant and the witnesses had been forced to make confessions was corroborated by the domestic courts in

Armenia: the police officers concerned were convicted there of ill-treatment. So the Court concluded that the use of such evidence rendered the trial of Mr Harutyunyan unfair and that there had been a clear violation of Article 6, paragraph 1 of the Convention (*Harutyunyan v. Armenia, 2007*).

## The right to silence

From the text of Article 6, paragraph 1, the Court has elaborated a right to silence which played an important part in the case brought by three Irishmen – Heaney, McGuinness and Quinn – against Ireland in December 2000.

> All three were arrested on suspicion of serious terrorist offences. When cautioned, they were told by police that they had a right to remain silent under the ECHR, but that under Section 52 of the Offences against the State Act (1939) they were nonetheless required to give details about their movements at the time of the relevant offences. All three refused to give an account of their movements and were sentenced to six months' imprisonment. Their appeal was based on the overriding right to a fair trial enshrined in Article 6 of the Convention, and specifically the right not to incriminate themselves.

**Article 6 –
Right to a fair trial**

In the determination of his civil rights and obligations or of any criminal charge against him, everyone is entitled to a fair and public hearing within a reasonable time by an independent and impartial tribunal established by law.

Everyone charged with a criminal offence shall be presumed innocent until proved guilty according to the law.

The Court found that imposing Section 52 of the Offences against the State Act, requiring those accused to answer questions when charged, destroyed the very essence of the privilege against self-incrimination and the right to remain silent. Even the serious security and public order concerns invoked by the Irish Government could not justify such a provision, and there had therefore been a violation of the applicants' rights as guaranteed by Article 6, paragraph 1. Moreover, given the close link with the presumption of innocence guaranteed by Article 6, paragraph 2, there had also been a violation of that provision (*Heaney and McGuinness v. Ireland* and *Quinn v. Ireland, 2000*).

Two high profile cases concerned the question

of whether media publicity may have affected the verdict of a trial. The judgments were given by the Court in 2002 and 2003. The first related to the chairman of the supervisory board of the largest Latvian bank after it was forced into liquidation, and the second related to the trial for corruption of the former Italian Prime Minister, Bettino Craxi.

## Presumption of innocence

In the politically charged time after the independence of Latvia from the Soviet Union in the early 1990s, the applicant was accused of economic sabotage, transferring millions of euros to a Russian bank in Moscow in exchange for worthless Russian government bonds, causing severe damage to the Latvian economy and financially ruining hundreds of thousands of small investors and depositors.

At his trial in 1997 the applicant suffered a heart attack in court. As a result, the preventive detention measures previously in force were relaxed, but the prime minister and the minister of justice at the time immediately published a statement in the press regretting this. The next day the judges dealing with the case also withdrew, quoting as a reason pressure "from the Government and the public", and the applicant's correspondence, including that with his lawyers, was seized and examined.

During his trial, the applicant on several occasions accused the presiding judge and the two other judges of bias. But at the prosecution's request an order for the presiding judge to withdraw was revoked by the Senate of the Supreme Court. The issue was referred to the Riga Regional Court, where – with the same judge presiding and the same two judges beside her – it was dismissed.

The presiding judge also made statements to the press criticising the conduct of the defence. She expressed her surprise that the applicant persisted in denying the charges, and called on him to prove his innocence. In a judgment in December 2001 the applicant was convicted and sentenced to nine years in prison.

The Court found that the Latvian authorities had not shown proper diligence in the conduct of proceedings for this case. The Court also found that the Riga Regional Court, to which the case was referred following the senate's ruling, was not correctly constituted. And the presiding judge's views, as expressed in the media, indicated a preference on her part for a guilty verdict, justifying the applicant questioning her impartiality. On all these counts the Court found there had been violations of Article 6. In addition, the presiding judge's statement to the press, asserting that the applicant should prove his innocence, was at variance with the principle of the presumption of innocence, one of the fundamental principles of a democratic state (*Lavents v. Latvia, 2002*).

## Politicians above the law?

Intense media interest surrounded the trial in Italy of Bennito Craxi, Secretary of the Italian Socialist Party and former prime minister, charged with false accounting, illegal funding of political parties, corruption and extortion. In what was known as the Eni-Sai case, Craxi and several co-defendants were charged with illegally bribing public officials and the directors of various companies involved. Bennito Craxi himself did not attend any of the 56 hearings in this trial. He remained in Tunisia, where he had fled, and was sentenced *in absentia* in December 1994 to five and a half years in prison.

The essence of his appeal to Strasbourg was that he had not had adequate time to prepare his defence and had been unable to cross-examine prosecution witnesses or to have them cross-examined. He further alleged that the press campaign conducted against him had influenced the judges determining his case.

As for not having adequate time to prepare his defence, the Court found that Craxi's lawyers had agreed dates of hearings in his absence and had not complained of time pressure until a month before sentence was passed. Hence they found no violation of Article 6 on that account.

The Court conceded that Craxi and his lawyers did not have an opportunity to cross-examine all witnesses, as one had died and others exercised their right to remain silent in court. Consequently they had not been in a position to challenge the pre-trial statements which formed the legal basis for the conviction. Here there was a violation of Craxi's rights under Article 6.

As for the interest of the media in the Eni-Sai case, the Court considered it inevitable that the press should comment on such matters, given the eminent position of the applicant, the political context, and the nature and gravity of the charges. There was, however, no evidence to suggest that the professional judges in this case had been influenced by statements made in the press. Hence it found no violation of Article 6 (*Craxi v. Italy, 2003*).

*Human Rights* by sculptor Mariano González Beltrán stands outside the Palais de l'Europe and represents society living in harmony with human rights.

## Frozen assets, easy terms, close relations?

A case that the Court considered in 2003 illustrates just how careful lawyers and judges must be when it comes to actions which might potentially compromise a fair trial.

> An applicant from Iceland, who had lost a case against the national bank there, discovered that the husband of one of the judges in the appeal case that he took to the Supreme Court in Reykjavik had been one of the guarantors of a debt to the national bank. The debtor had defaulted, and to meet his guarantee the husband had mortgaged two properties owned by his wife, the judge. Subsequently, in a generous gesture, 75% of the husband's guarantee was forgone by the national bank. The applicant complained that, on account of the close financial relationship between the judge and her husband on the one hand and the National Bank of Iceland on the other, his case against the bank had not been heard by an independent and impartial tribunal as required by Article 6 of the Convention.

The Court observed there was no evidence to suggest the judge had been personally biased, and the sums involved were not so large as to be likely to affect her impartiality. Nonetheless the coincidence of the appeal to the Supreme Court occurring at the same time as the favourable financial settlement with the judge's husband could reasonably have led the applicant to fear that the Supreme Court was not impartial. Hence the judgment of the Court was in the applicant's favour; there had been a violation of his right to a fair trial (*Petur Thor Sigurdsson v. Iceland, 2003*).

## No punishment without law

The fall of the Berlin Wall brought down the legal order that the Communist party had imposed in each of the states of central and eastern Europe. The effect of this is still felt across that half of the continent, as the democratic legal structures of the successor states take root in newly free societies. Legal structures in the new states have to come to terms with acts committed under the previous regime, affecting both property and persons. The effects of this have been felt most starkly in reunified Germany where some of the perpetrators of human rights abuses under the previous regime in the German Democratic Republic (GDR – "East Germany" ) were subsequently brought to justice.

> The most high profile case of this sort before the Court was that of Fritz Streletz, Heinz Kessler and Egon Krenz, three former senior East German officials (respectively a deputy minister of defence, a minister of defence and the president of the council of state of the GDR) and a former East German border guard. All four applicants were convicted by the courts of the Federal Republic of Germany ("West Germany") after German reunification in 1990. The three officials were convicted of participating at the highest level in the political decisions that ordered a shoot-to-kill policy for GDR citizens attempting to flee across the inner-German border. The border guard was convicted of firing the fatal shot in one particular instance.

The applicants appealed on the grounds that when they committed their actions, they were not offences under the law of the GDR or under international law, and that their conviction in the German courts breached Article 7, paragraph 1, of the ECHR.

In this case, the Court referred to the principles enshrined in the GDR's own constitution which expressly included the need to preserve human life. The reason of state invoked by the GDR – to protect the borders of the GDR "at all costs" in order to save the GDR from a massive outflow of its own population – had to be limited by the principles enunciated in the GDR's own constitution and also in its legislation. Actual practice at the borders was regulated by secret orders and service instructions were not published in the Official Gazette, but were known to the applicants, who had themselves helped to draw them up, making them directly responsible for the situation at the border between the two German states.

## Article 7 – No punishment without law

No one shall be held guilty of any criminal offence on account of any act or omission which did not constitute a criminal offence under national or international law at the time when it was committed. Nor shall a heavier penalty be imposed than the one that was applicable at the time the criminal offence was committed.

The Court considered that it was legitimate for a state governed by the rule of law, such as the FRG, to bring criminal proceedings against persons who had committed crimes under a former regime. The Court also considered that the GDR's border-policing policy, which flagrantly infringed human rights and above all the right to life, could not be covered by the protection of Article 7, paragraph 1, of the Convention. The actual exercise of policing the border in the GDR, in particular the shoot-to-kill policy, emptied of its substance the legislation on which it was supposed to be based.

Hence the Court ruled that the conviction of the applicants by the German courts after reunification had not breached Article 7, paragraph 1 (*Streletz, Kessler and Krenz v. Germany, 2001*).

## Right of appeal and compensation for wrongful conviction

The ECHR also provides for a right of appeal in criminal matters and for compensation for wrongful conviction, as well as the right not to be tried or punished twice for the same offence in the same state. These additional rights were added to the ECHR by way of Protocol No.7 in 1984, strengthening the right to a fair trial with three additional articles.

# Privacy and family life

This right is susceptible to extensive interpretation, and the Court has been careful not to define at all strictly the boundaries of its application. In different judgments it has defined private life to include "activities of a professional or business nature", the "right to establish and develop relationships with other human beings and the outside world", "a zone of interaction of a person with others, even in a public context", the "physical and psychological integrity of a person", the "right to personal development", and "the right to establish details of their identity as human beings". One commentator suggests: "Interests as diverse as the right to live as a gypsy, to change one's name and to be free from environmental pollution, as well as more traditional 'privacy' rights such as protection against dissemination of personal information and images all fall within it."

Within the Court's case law relating to this article one can identify five specific "freedoms" – three "freedoms from" and two "freedoms to". The three are the right to be free from interference with one's physical and psychological integrity, from unwanted access to and collection of information, and from serious environmental pollution affecting an individual's health. The two are the right to be free to develop one's personality and identity, and the freedom to live your life the way you want to.

## Article 8 – Right to respect for private and family life

Everyone has the right to respect for his private and family life, his home and his correspondence.

The Court interprets the ECHR in a dynamic manner, adjusting the balance between competing rights in the light of changing circumstances. The case law of the Court has shown an increasing tendency over recent years to prioritise the protection of privacy over freedom of expression. This causes concern in media circles, especially among journalists who fear their task of exposing wrong-doing may be hampered by greater protection of privacy.

The Court's earlier robust defence of press freedom now appears to be weakening in favour of a more extensive protection of personal privacy, as the following case demonstrates.

## Public interest or of interest to the public?

After several cases that she lost in the German courts over a period of 10 years, Princess Caroline of Hanover finally appealed to the European Court of Human Rights against a particular judgment concerning photographs taken without her consent in France and published in Germany. Under German law, Princess Caroline is considered a "public figure" and as such the public is deemed to have a legitimate interest in knowing how she behaves in public, even when not performing any official function. The photographs in question showed her going about everyday tasks – shopping, playing sport, collecting her children from school.

The German authorities claimed that the level of protection afforded to such a figure under German law was compatible with Article 8, balancing it with the right to freedom of expression enshrined in Article 10.

In its judgment, however, the European Court of Human Rights concluded that the protection of family life "extends beyond the private family circle and also includes a social dimension. The Court considers that anyone, even if they are known to the general public, must be able to enjoy a legitimate expectation of protection of and respect for their private life". The majority of judges added that the question of the correct balance between Articles 8 and 10 centred on "the contribution that the published photos and articles make to a debate of general interest". In the case of Princess Caroline, the photographs made no such contribution as she exercised no official function and the photographs related solely to her private life (*von Hannover v. Germany, 2004*).

## Is CCTV in public places an intrusion into privacy?

A similar line was taken by the Court in 2003 as regards the broadcast of CCTV footage in the UK showing a young man on a public street attempting to commit suicide. The local authority concerned used the material to show the effectiveness of the CCTV system it had installed to prevent or detect crime, and the footage was re-broadcast by regional and national broadcasters. Despite blurring the image of his face in the broadcasts, neighbours, colleagues, friends and family who saw the programmes recognised the applicant.

The Court found there was a breach of Article 8 in this case. The applicant was in a public street but not for the purpose of participating in any public event. If the local authority wanted to advertise the effectiveness of its system, it could have done so by other means. The disclosure of the young man's identity represented a disproportionate, and therefore unjustified, interference with his private life (*Peck v. the United Kingdom, 2003*).

## What's in a name?

Most people do not mind what other people call their pets, but it seems quite reasonable that children should be protected from being called unsuitable names by their parents. Hence most countries have legislation in place which recognises that national name practice is in the public interest. It permits common or traditional names and excludes invented or outlandish ones.

> In 1999 the Finnish authorities refused to register "Axl" as a forename for a boy, even though the name was used in the family and did not differ very much from other short forenames such as "Alf" and "Ulf" also used commonly in Finland. The family appealed to the European Court of Human Rights, alleging a violation of Article 8, the right to respect for family life, and the Court found in their favour.

The Court concluded the name was not whimsical or ridiculous, nor was it likely to prejudice the child as it grew up. It could be pronounced in Finnish and was also used in some other countries. According to the official Population Information System it was already in use in Finland, though rarely, with just three other persons with that name registered. The authorities conceded that this had no negative consequences for the preservation of the cultural and linguistic identity of the country. Game, set and match to the family (*Johansson v. Finland, 2007*)!

## The marrying sort

There have been major social changes in the institution of marriage since the Convention was adopted. The straightforward language of Article 12 must now be related to a range of issues dealing with the increasingly common phenomena of cohabitation, divorce, same sex partnerships and transsexuality, as well as adapted to the developing nature of the core institution itself. The following cases illustrate some of these issues.

## Jailbirds, lovebirds?

Thirty years ago two separate cases raised the issue of a prisoner's right to marry.

> In the Hamer case and the Draper case the applicants complained that they were each prevented from marrying while they were serving their sentences in jail (and one of them was serving a life sentence). At that time UK law did not permit marriages in prison and the UK authorities refused to allow a prisoner a temporary release so that he or she could be married elsewhere.

The Court upheld the prisoners' complaints as violations of Article 12, and

**Article 12 – Right to marry**

Men and women of marriageable age have the right to marry and to found a family, according to the national laws governing the exercise of this right.

the UK Government subsequently changed the domestic law and prison procedures, allowing prisoners to solemnise their marriage at their home. The Court commented in its judgment that the essence of the right to marry is the formation of a legally binding association between a man and a woman. It is for them to decide whether or not they wish to enter such an association in circumstances where they cannot cohabit (*Hamer v. the United Kingdom, 1979* and *Draper v. the United Kingdom, 1980*).

## Frequent marriage, frequent divorce

> In 1987 a Swiss court banned a Swiss national from marrying again for three years after his third divorce.

The decision was in line with the Swiss Civil Code at the time, which – alone among the member states of the Council of Europe – maintained this provision in its legislation. He appealed to the Court against this judgment, which found in his favour.

The Court reasoned that the exercise of the fundamental right to marry, enshrined in Article 12, gives rise to personal, social and legal consequences for the individuals concerned, and is also subject to national laws. But the limitations introduced in that way must not restrict or reduce the very essence of the right itself. While the Court recognised that the Swiss ban served the interests of marital stability, it ruled that the means chosen by the Swiss authorities were disproportionate to the aim pursued. Thus the right of a divorced person to remarry has to be without unreasonable restrictions (*F. v. Switzerland, 1987*).

## Marriage between in-laws

In 2005 B and L, a father-in-law and a daughter-in-law, wanted to marry. Under United Kingdom law marriage between a father-in-law and his daughter-in-law while their former spouses are still alive used not to be permitted. Admittedly this is not a common situation, but at that time the individuals concerned had to apply to parliament for a dispensation, an exceptional and costly procedure, not subject to any discernable rules or precedent. They took their case to the European Court of Human Rights, alleging that the ban on their marrying under UK law was a violation of Article 12.

The Court observed that the bar to marriage between in-laws, although pursuing a legitimate aim in protecting the integrity of the family, did not prevent such relationships occurring. No incest or criminal law provisions prevented extra-marital relationships between parents-in-law and children-in-law. In previous cases the UK parliament had waived the bar when it appeared that it served no useful purpose of public policy. The stated aim of the bar – and the waiver applied in some cases – undermined the rationality and the logic of the law in question.

So the Court concluded that there had been, in the circumstances of this case, a violation of Article 12 of the Convention: B and L could marry, and the UK had to revise its legislation (*B. and L. v. the United Kingdom, 2005*).

## Transsexuals' right to marry

Complex issues were raised by a complaint from Christine Goodwin, a post-operative male-to-female transsexual from Britain, that her rights had been infringed in relation to both Article 8 (respect for family and private life) and Article 12 (right to marry). She claimed she faced sexual harassment at work because she was unable to change her legal status from man to woman. This also affected her national insurance payments, her social security entitlements, her prospective date of retirement and her right to marry.

The Court asserted that there was clear and uncontested evidence of a continuing international trend in favour of increased social acceptance of transsexuals and also of legal recognition of the new social identity of post-operative transsexuals. Third parties would not suffer any material prejudice from possible changes to the birth register that might flow from allowing recognition of gender reassignment.

In this case the applicant lived as a woman, would wish to marry a man, and yet had no possibility of doing so. She could therefore claim that the very essence of her right to marry had been infringed. Though fewer countries permitted the marriage of transsexuals in their assigned gender than recognised the change of gender itself, the Court did not find that this supported an argument for leaving the matter entirely within the individual state's margin of appreciation. States could determine the conditions under which transsexuals establish that gender reassignment has been properly effected and the formalities applicable to future marriages, but the Court found no justification for barring transsexuals from enjoying the right to marry. Hence the Court did find violations both of Article 8 and Article 12 in this case (*Christine Goodwin v. the United Kingdom, 2002*).

## Equality between spouses

Protocol No.7 to the ECHR, which was agreed by the member states in 1984, introduced not only several additional rights concerning legal practice – the right of appeal, compensation for wrongful conviction and the right not to be punished twice for the same offence – but also the notion of equality between spouses.

Perhaps it will come as a surprise to the general reader that this protocol, which contains the short article relating to the equality of spouses, has not been ratified over the intervening years by a number of member states, including Belgium, Germany, the Netherlands, Spain, Turkey and the United Kingdom, and so remains something of a dead letter. Despite this, there clearly are issues at stake where both immigrants and indigenous people of Muslim belief are confronted with the widespread emancipation of women in contemporary European society. Sharia law maintains a very different view of woman's role, particularly in marriage, from that which has developed in the rest of society, and behind that distinction lies the opposition between faith in a divine and a secular source of law.

> **Protocol No.7, Article 5 – Equality between spouses**
>
> Spouses shall enjoy equality of rights and responsibilities of a private law character between them, and in their relations with their children, as to marriage, during marriage and in the event of its dissolution. This Article shall not prevent states from taking such measures as are necessary in the interests of the children.

In a case where the Welfare Party (Refah Partisi) appealed to the Court of Human Rights against the ban imposed on it by the Turkish Constitutional Court, the Strasbourg Court observed:

> It is difficult to declare one's respect for democracy and human rights while at the same time supporting a regime based on sharia, which clearly diverges from Convention values, particularly with regard to its criminal law and criminal procedure, its rules on the legal status of women and the way it intervenes in all spheres of private and public life with religious precepts.

The Court wen t on to maintain the ban, adding:

> In the Court's view, a political party whose actions seem to be aimed at introducing sharia in a State Party to the Convention can hardly be regarded as an association complying with the democratic ideal that underlies the whole Convention.

# Freedom of thought, conscience and religion

European history is marked by the sufferings of those who have died for their beliefs. Christian martyrs in pagan times, pagans slaughtered in the name of Christianity, heretics killed by Catholics, and Catholics killed by Protestants, pogroms of Jews and the burning of witches, always those of another persuasion, drowned, hanged, burned or butchered with excessive zeal by those who thought they knew better. One of the greatest achievements of the Enlightenment was to encourage a spirit of tolerance that has progressively marked law-making in Europe since the end of the 18th century. After the Second World War, those who drafted the Convention stood firmly in that tradition of toleration, scarred as they were with the recent history of secular intolerance as well, where the rights of ideological enemies and those of other races and nations were abused with excessive barbarity by communists and fascists alike.

Article 9 of the Convention regarding freedom of thought, conscience and religion, along with the following two articles that relate to freedom of expression and freedom of assembly and association, address this issue. The Court's dynamic interpretation of the Convention in this respect applies them to contemporary issues in a way that reflects their central importance in protecting human rights in a continent that is changing quickly in the light of demographic, social and cultural developments.

## Wearing an Islamic headscarf

> In 2004 the Court gave judgment in an important case concerning a ban issued by the Vice Chancellor of Istanbul University on students wearing Islamic headscarves. Leyla Sahin, a fifth year medical student, was refused access to a written examination because she was wearing the Islamic headscarf. The ban was based on a circular issued by the Vice Chancellor, directing that students with beards and students wearing the Islamic headscarf would be refused admission to lectures, courses and tutorials.

The Court came to the conclusion that, although the circular at issue did constitute an interference with the applicant's right to manifest her religion, it had been "prescribed by law", as mentioned in paragraph 2 of Article 9, and so the interference with this right was in this case justified.

The Court noted that the Turkish Constitutional Court had earlier ruled that authorising students to cover the neck and hair with a veil or headscarf for reasons of religious conviction was contrary to the secular constitution. The Supreme Administrative Court had also held that wearing the Islamic headscarf at university was not compatible with the fundamental principles of the republic. So the European Court of Human Rights found that there was a legal basis for this interference in Turkish law, and the applicant could and should have been aware of this, since regulations on this existed at the university since long before she enrolled there.

As to whether the interference was necessary, the Court noted that it was based in particular on principles of secularism and equality. According to the case law of the Constitutional Court, secularism, as a guarantee of democratic

## Article 9 – Freedom of thought, conscience and religion

1. Everyone has the right to freedom of thought, conscience and religion; this right includes freedom to change his religion or belief and freedom, either alone or in community with others and in public or private, to manifest his religion or belief, in worship, teaching, practice and observance.

2. Freedom to manifest one's religion or beliefs shall be subject only to such limitations as are prescribed by law and are necessary in a democratic society in the interests of public safety, for the protection of public order, health or morals, or for the protection of the rights and freedoms of others.

values, ensured both liberty and equality. This principle prevented the state from showing preference for any one particular religion or belief. It guided the state as an impartial arbiter, and necessarily entailed freedom of religion and conscience for all.

Article 9 also involved protection of the rights and freedoms of others and the maintenance of public order, and these goals were served by this ban as well. As many other students chose not to wear the headscarf, there was potential conflict with extremist political movements in Turkey which sought to impose on society as a whole their religious symbols and a conception of society founded on religious precepts (*Leyla Sahin v. Turkey, 2004*).

## Swearing on the Bible

San Marino, a member of the Council of Europe, is a micro-state, tucked away in the middle of Italy. It was founded back in the mists of time by a Christian saint, and the issue of the Christian nature of the state came to the fore in a case on which the Court gave judgment in 1999.

Two parliamentarians who were elected in June 1993 to the San Marino Parliament – the Consiglio Grande et Generale – took their oath of office in writing, omitting the reference to the Bible required by the Elections Act. Parliament ordered the deputies to take the oath again, this time swearing on the Bible, on pain of forfeiting their seats. They complied, but complained that their right to freedom of religion and conscience had been infringed.

The San Marino Government must have quickly realised the error of its ways because it changed the law, introducing an option for deputies to swear in future "on my honour" as an alternative to swearing on the Bible. But the European Court of Human Rights considered the applicants' complaints nonetheless, and the ruling is of some interest.

In its defence, the San Marino Government stressed the importance of the oath, the special character of San Marino's history and national traditions, closely linked to Christianity since the founding of the republic. It asserted, however, that the religious significance of the oath had been replaced now by "the need to preserve public order, in the form of social cohesion and the citizens' trust in their traditional institutions".

The Court accepted that in general San Marino's laws guaranteed freedom of conscience and religion, but in this case requiring the applicants to take the oath on the Bible had been tantamount to requiring two representatives of the people to swear allegiance to a particular religion. That was not compatible with Article 9 of the Convention. It was contradictory to make the exercise of an elected mandate, intended to represent different views of society within parliament, subject to a prior declaration of commitment to a particular set of beliefs. Such a limitation could not be regarded as "necessary in a democratic society" (*Buscarini and others v. San Marino, 1999*).

## Sacked for religious beliefs

Against a background of intense religious proselytising in central and eastern Europe after the fall of communism, several states were reluctant to register Christian evangelical groups officially. Legal status would facilitate their access to services such as hiring meeting halls and opening bank accounts. In Bulgaria one such group – Word of Life – was refused registration and operated clandestinely.

A Bulgarian applicant, Kalinka Todorova Ivanova, claimed she was sacked from her post as a swimming pool manager at the River Shipbuilding and Navigation School in Ruse in Bulgaria because she was a member of Word of Life. First Ms Ivanova's principal at the Ruse school was dismissed by the Ministry of Education for, among other things, having tolerated Word of Life's activities at the school. Then Ms Ivanova was put under pressure to resign or renounce her faith. The chief education inspector for Ruse and his deputy were alleged to have threatened that they would otherwise instruct the new principal to dismiss her. She refused, and a month later she was dismissed "because she no longer met the educational and professional requirements of the post". Appeals against her dismissal were all rejected, in the District Court, the Regional Court an d the Supreme Court of Cassation. So she took her case to the European Court of Human Rights.

The Bulgarian Government was concerned to maintain the secular nature of the education system and quoted to the Court alleged instances of proselytising at the Ruse school by staff members there. But it did not provide evidence that Ms Ivanova had been directly involved; indeed it argued that her dismissal had nothing to do with her religious beliefs. By considering the sequence of events in their entirety, including the broader context of the authorities' antipathy to Word of Life, the Court concluded, however, that she had been sacked essentially because of her affiliation with Word of Life. The fact that she had been dismissed in accordance with the applicable labour law did not eliminate the substantive motive for her dismissal (*Ivanova v. Bulgaria, 2007*).

# Freedom of expression

It was Thomas Jefferson who said at the time of the American Revolution that he would rather live under a corrupt government so long as the press was free, than under an honest government with a corrupt press. In the first case, he argued, the public would get at the truth some time and put matters right; in the second, they would never know if it ever went wrong. So it is not surprising that Article 10 of the ECHR – freedom of expression – has often been invoked by journalists when the state has abused their right to reveal the truth about bad government.

It is not only journalists who have used this article as a guarantee of their right to freedom of expression, as the following selection of cases shows. But in a democratic society we all rely heavily on the media for our day-to-day knowledge of government and politics and of society more generally. Those who work in the media have a particular responsibility to inform the wider public. Their activity, for all that it carries duties and responsibilities with it, requires the special protection afforded by this article.

## Article 10 – Freedom of expression

Everyone has the right to freedom of expression. This right shall include freedom to hold opinions and ideas without interference by public authority and regardless of frontiers. This article shall not prevent states from requiring the licensing of broadcasting, television or cinema enterprises.

## Revealing state secrets

First the facts. Two NGOs in Dublin provided women with information on pregnancy-related options including abortion facilities abroad. Since abortion was a criminal offence in that country, the Irish Supreme Court issued an injunction forbidding the two organisations from providing information to pregnant women about the location, name or even the telephone numbers of abortion clinics in Britain.

Then the judgment. Even if Ireland had a legitimate interest in protecting the life of the unborn, argued the Court, the injunction had a disproportionate effect. It prohibited counselling regardless of the age, health or circumstances of pregnant women, and posed a health risk to women who might in consequence terminate pregnancies at a later stage without adequate counselling.

The Court refused to take into account Article 2 of the ECHR (right to life) – as requested by the Irish Government – since the NGOs did not claim that the Convention contains a right to abortion, but merely that their right to provide and receive information concerning abortion abroad was at stake (*Open Door and Dublin Well Woman v. Ireland, 1992*).

## Journalists and their sources

Several cases before the Court have concerned the right of journalists not to reveal their sources. For journalists, indeed for the freedom of the media as a whole, this is an important issue. Revealing sources may have serious, perhaps even fatal, consequences for those who give information to journalists. It also ruins the reputation of the journalist or publication concerned as a safe repository of confidential information. The journalist's career and the publisher's future – in extreme cases even their lives – can thus be put at risk.

Judges at the European Court of Human Rights

> As recently as 2007, a Dutch journalist was detained for more than two weeks, in the Netherlands, to force him to reveal his sources among the Amsterdam police in a case of arms trafficking. He had written a critical article about the initial police investigation, but refused to reveal his source when asked to do so on the witness stand by the Court of Appeal, which subsequently ordered his detention for contempt of court.

When his appeal reached Strasbourg, the Court recalled its view that the protection of a journalist's sources was one of the basic conditions for freedom of the press. The Council of Europe's Committee of Ministers had issued a recommendation to this effect only a few months before the events in this case. Without such protection, it reminded the member states, sources might be deterred from assisting the press in informing the public on matters of public interest and the vital public watchdog role of the press could be undermined. The order to disclose a source could only be justified by an overriding requirement in the public interest.

In this case, the Court remarked on the lengths to which the Dutch authorities had gone to learn just who inside the Amsterdam police force had leaked information to the journalist. Such far-reaching measures, it asserted, could only discourage those who had true and accurate information about criminal activity from sharing their knowledge with the press in the future. The Court concluded that the government's interest in knowing the identity of the applicant's source was not sufficient to override the applicant's interest in concealing it (*Voskuil v. the Netherlands, 2007*).

## Arbitrary action against an investigative journalist

Barely a week after its judgment in the Voskuil case, the Court delivered another judgment relating to Article 10 in the case of a German journalist working in Brussels to cover events in the European Union.

> In 2002, Hans Martin Tillack published two articles in *Stern* magazine reporting allegations of a European civil servant regarding financial irregularities in the EU institutions and the ensuing investigation by the European Anti-Fraud Office (OLAF). After an internal investigation in the EU institutions revealed no actionable wrong-doing, OLAF lodged a complaint against the journalist with the Belgian authorities. The police opened an investigation for breach of professional confidence and possible bribery involving a civil servant. Two years after publication of the articles in *Stern*, police searched the journalist's flat and office, seized his computers, his mobile phones and working papers. Despite repeated requests, they refused to return them.

When the case reached the Court in Strasbourg, it reiterated the principle that the protection of journalistic sources was a basic condition for press freedom. The interference by the Belgian authorities was not "necessary in a democratic society". The right of a journalist not to reveal his or her sources cannot be considered a mere privilege to be granted or taken away depending on the lawfulness or unlawfulness of his or her sources. It is part and parcel of the right to information, to be treated with the utmost caution. Even if the reasons given by the Belgian courts were "relevant", they were not "sufficient" to justify the searches (*Tillack v. Belgium, 2007*).

## Insulting or just embarrassing publications?

Just how far VIPs can shield themselves from journalistic reporting that is in the public interest was illustrated by a case against France brought to the Court in Strasbourg by the publishing director of *Le Monde* in 2002.

In 1995 the newspaper published an article on drug trafficking in Morocco which implicated King Hassan II and his entourage. The king brought a case on the basis of an 1881 French law on the freedom of the press, one section of which was concerned with insulting a foreign head of state.

The defendants were initially acquitted by the Paris Criminal Court, but King Hassan appealed against the judgment, and the Paris Court of Appeal found in his favour. A counter-appeal to the Criminal Division of the Court of Cassation by the defendants was dismissed, and the publishers of *Le Monde* then appealed to the European Court of Human Rights. They objected to the provision of the French law as an abuse of their human rights under Article 10.

The Strasbourg Court found that there was legitimate public interest in the issue discussed in the article, based as it was on a report for the European Union – which Morocco at that time had applied to join – about drug production and trafficking in that country. It stated that the media had to act in good faith on an accurate factual basis and provide reliable and precise information in accordance with the ethics of journalism. They should be able to rely on official reports and not have to carry out their own separate investigations into the matter.

The Court also noted that, even if the allegations in the report – and the subsequent article based on it – were true, this particular French law did not allow journalists to use this fact in their defence. Prosecution under this law was a disproportionate means of protecting the reputation of VIPs. The law on defamation – where the veracity of the articles would have been a pertinent fact – should have been a sufficient safeguard for their reputations.

The Court also noted that conferring special legal status on heads of state could not be reconciled with modern practice and political conceptions. Immunity from criticism solely on account of status or function, irrespective of whether the criticism was justified, was a privilege that went beyond what was necessary to achieve the objective. The Court found that there was no reasonable proportion between the restrictions imposed on the journalist's or the publisher's freedom of expression and the legitimate aim pursued. France lost and *Le Monde* won (*Colombani and others v. France, 2002*).

## Freedom of assembly and association

The right of assembly and association may seem at first sight to be so uncontested nowadays that we take it for granted. But, as with so many human rights, taking them for granted is often the quickest way to lose them. The issue crops up in several strange ways and in many different countries, as the following cases illustrate.

## Masonic secrecy and public office

> The Grande Oriente d'Italia di Palazzo Guistiniani is an Italian Masonic association which groups together several lodges. It has been in existence since 1805. In 2001, it complained to the European Court of Human Rights that a regional law in Friuli-Venezia Giulia required candidates for public office to declare whether they were a member of a Masonic or, in any event, a secret organisation. The absence of a declaration constituted a ground for refusing appointment. This requirement, it argued, was discriminatory and incompatible with its right to freedom of association, guaranteed in Article 11 of the ECHR.

The Court noted that the law in question made a distinction between secret organisations (including Masonic lodges) and others where membership was not secret. It also noted that the prohibition on nominating Freemasons to certain public offices for which the region was the appointing authority was not "necessary in a democratic society". Penalising someone for their membership of an association – secret or not – was unjustified, since that fact was not in itself reprehensible (*Grande Oriente d'Italia di Palazzo Giustiniani v. Italy [No. 2], 2001*).

## Workers' rights and the closed shop

Two applicants – a student and a gardener – won a joint case at the Court in 2007 on the issue of the "closed shop", a practice where employment with a particular firm requires membership of a particular trade union.

> Each of the applicants was required to join a trade union called SID, affiliated to the Danish Confederation of Trade Unions, in order to obtain their jobs. The former applicant, a student, was a holiday relief worker for a distribution company; the latter worked as a gardener. In 1996 the student refused to join the trade union and was dismissed from his job the next day. In 1999 the gardener joined, but under protest, stating that he did not agree with the political views of the union.

In the view of the Court, Article 11 encompasses a negative right not to be forced to join an association as well as a positive right to join one. It acknowledged that states enjoy a wide margin of appreciation concerning the freedom of trade unions to protect the occupational interests of their members.

But it also noted that the Danish Government had twice tried – unsuccessfully – to pass legislation reforming the "closed shop" legislation. While the individual right of both applicants to freedom of association had been infringed, the Court also found that there was little support in European society generally for the maintenance of "closed shop" arrangements, only Denmark and Iceland doing so at the time. To the Court this was an indication that "closed shop" agreements in the labour market were not an indispensable tool for the effective enjoyment of trade union freedoms. The individuals in question won their case, and Denmark was required to revise its legislation (*Sørensen and Rasmussen v. Denmark, 2007*).

## Education: lessons from the state?

The first protocol to amend the ECHR was agreed in 1952 and one of the key articles in it relates to the right to education.

Education plays such a central role in people's lives, both as children or as parents, that it is unsurprising the Court's case law underlines the importance of the state in its provision. This issue of the nature of the state's input came to the fore in an early case concerning sex education, where the Court ruled that the nature of the state's responsibility in this field was to ensure that:

> information or knowledge included in the curriculum is conveyed in an objective, critical and pluralistic manner. The state is forbidden to pursue an aim of indoctrination that might be considered as not respecting parents' religious and philosophical convictions. This is a limit that must not be exceeded (*Kjeldsen, Busk Madsen and Pedersen v. Denmark, 1976*).

The Court has also upheld the right of parents and others to provide private education outside the state system, but has refrained from absolving the state of its responsibilities in this field, as otherwise the provision of education would be the preserve only of those who could afford to pay for it.

## Protocol 1, Article 2 – Right to education

No person shall be denied the right to education. In the exercise of any functions which it assumes in relation to education and to teaching, the State shall respect the right of parents to ensure such education and teaching in conformity with their own religious and philosophical convictions.

Behind one of the rare cases where one member state has taken another to the Court hovered just such a fear of the exclusion of some children from education.

> Greek Cypriot children living in Northern Cyprus were denied education after the Turkish-speaking authorities there closed down educational establishments for the children of Greek Cypriots. They argued that they could travel to the South to school, but then made it difficult for them to return to their homes in the North. Cyprus took Turkey to the Court.

The Court condemned Turkey for disproportionately restricting the enjoyment of the right to family life as the price for the enjoyment of the right to education (*Cyprus v. Turkey, 2001*).

In a case on the vexed issue of corporal punishment in schools the Court enunciated a clear distinction between education and teaching which has guided its judgments in this area:

> The education of children is the whole process whereby, in any society, adults endeavour to transmit their beliefs, culture and other values to the young, whereas teaching or instruction refers in particular to the transmission of knowledge and to intellectual development.

While the right to education calls for regulation by the state, said the Court, that regulation must not injure the substance of the rights of parents to ensure that education is in conformity with their beliefs. In this case, their opposition to corporal punishment won the day, and since then corporal punishment is not administered in state schools (*Campbell and Cosans v. the United Kingdom, 1982*).

## Free elections

If you live in a stable democracy you might think that it is superfluous for the ECHR to include an article on the right to free elections. But for very good reasons the first protocol, negotiated by the member states and opened for signature in 1952, also contained just such an article. By then the Iron Curtain had come down across Europe – "From Stettin on the Baltic to Trieste on the Adriatic," as Churchill eloquently expressed it – dividing the continent into a democratic West and a totalitarian East. The member states of the Council of Europe were reinforcing the parliamentary and democratic nature of their part of Europe by enshrining in this text the right of the people to "hold free elections at reasonable intervals by secret ballot". That was a right clearly denied to those living in de facto one-party communist states to their east.

Member states have found themselves arraigned in the Court for violations of this article for a multitude of different reasons, for example for excluding some of their territory from an electoral franchise, for preventing certain candidates from standing for election, or for denying some of their citizens the right to vote.

## Gibraltar and the European elections

A British citizen resident in Gibraltar applied in 1994 to register as a voter in elections to the European Parliament but was refused on the grounds that the UK franchise for the elections did not include that territory. Attempts to amend the UK legislation relating to the elections were defeated by the British Government itself in the House of Lords in 1998.

The Court ruled in favour of the applicant and against the UK the following year. Attempts by Spain to reverse this decision through the European Union's Court of Justice failed, and as a result Gibraltar was included in the franchise for UK elections to the European Parliament as from 2004 (*Matthews v. the United Kingdom, 1999*).

## Voting from behind bars

A prisoner argued that the UK law depriving him of the right to vote because he was a convicted felon was incompatible with Article 3 of Protocol No. 1 of the ECHR. Seven judges, sitting as a Chamber of the Court (see next section on how the Court works) declared unanimously that there had been a violation of his rights, but the United Kingdom appealed to the Grand Chamber of 17 judges where the judgment was more nuanced. Twelve of them found that there had been a violation, but five did not. As yet, UK law has not been amended to allow prisoners to vote, but a public debate is now underway in Britain and may presage a change in the law at a later date (*Hirst v. the United Kingdom, 2005*).

## Language tests for parliamentary candidates

In Latvia, where there is a large Russian-speaking minority, candidates for public office are required to prove that they are competent in the Latvian language.

In 1998, Mrs Podkolzina was included in a list of candidates submitted to the electoral authorities by the National Harmony Party, and her application was accompanied by a certificate of linguistic competence in Latvian. However, a state language examiner subsequently visited Mrs Podkolzina and reported that she did not command Latvian at the "third level", the highest level defined in Latvian regulations and required for eligibility for parliament. The Electoral Commission subsequently struck her name off the list. The party asked the Riga Regional Court to set aside the Electoral Commission's decision, but the Court held there had been no breach of the law, and Mrs Podkolzina could not stand for election.

**Protocol 1, Article 3 – Right to free elections**

The High Contracting Parties undertake to hold free elections at reasonable intervals by secret ballot, under conditions which will ensure the free expression of the opinion of the people in the choice of the legislature.

So she appealed to the European Court of Human Rights and the Court found in her favour. The Latvian authorities had never questioned the validity of Mrs Podkolzina's original certificate and had subjected her to an arbitrary additional inspection by a single examiner exercising "exorbitant power". The Riga Regional Court had been remiss in not considering the original certificate, which had been issued after an examination by a board of five examiners, and relying instead solely on the report of the single inspector. That procedure had lacked "the fundamental guarantees of fairness" (*Podkolzina v. Latvia, 2002*).

# Discrimination

Central to the notion of human rights is the idea that each person must be able to take advantage of these rights on an equal footing with other people, without suffering discrimination. Article 14 of the ECHR protects against discrimination based on sex, race, colour, language, religion and several other criteria. These grounds are not strictly defined, so that the Court retains the flexibility to interpret them in the light of changing circumstances.

The article safeguards individuals who are in similar situations from any discrimination in the enjoyment of the rights and freedoms spelled out in the ECHR. Article 14 has no independent existence, but it plays an important role by complementing the provisions of the Convention and its protocols. It cannot be invoked as an article standing on its own; it must be presented alongside another article referring to a right provided by the Convention. Therefore a measure which violates a given right or freedom and is discriminatory is said to have violated the two articles cited "in conjunction".

### Article 14 – Prohibition of discrimination

The enjoyment of the rights and freedoms set forth in this Convention shall be secured without discrimination on any ground such as sex, race, colour, language, religion, political or other opinion, national or social origin, association with a national minority, birth or other status.

One recent case involving Article 14 that was subject to much media coverage was the banning of a lesbian, gay, bisexual, transgender parade in Warsaw in 2005. The Court held that the ban issued by the Mayor of Warsaw (who subsequently was elected president of Poland) was in violation of Articles 11 and 14 of the Convention, as other parades due to take place on the same day were not banned. The ruling was the first to affirm that banning such parades, simply due to their nature, was discriminatory, a violation on grounds of discrimination in conjunction with the right to freedom of assembly and association (*Baczkowski and Others v. Poland, 2007*).

Discrimination is defined as a distinction that is not founded on objective and reasonable criteria. However, the converse is also true, that a distinction founded on objective and reasonable criteria is not discrimination and does not violate Article 14. Making such assessments is a subjective operation that calls upon the Court to make value judgments in areas of intense cultural and social concern.

In the "Belgian Linguistics" case of 1968, regarding the provision of French education in Flemish regions of Belgium, the Court explained that:

> Article 14 ... does not prohibit distinctions in treatment which are founded on an objective assessment of essentially different factual circumstances and which, being based on the public interest, strike a fair balance between the protection of the interests of the community and respect for the rights and freedoms safeguarded by the Convention.

There is no obligation on a member state to apply different treatment in distinct situations, but if member states do not provide different treatment to people in distinct situations without an objective and reasonable justification, they may suffer discrimination nonetheless.

> A case on which the Court gave judgment in 2000 rested on a series of events which began in the 1980s. A Greek national, who was a Jehovah's Witness, refused on grounds of conscience to do military service. In December 1983 the Permanent Martial Court found him guilty of insubordination for refusing to enlist in the army for religious reasons and he was sent to prison. Several years later, after his release, the executive board of the Greek chartered accountants' body refused to appoint him as a chartered accountant because he had a criminal record, even though he had passed the relevant qualifying examination. The applicant appealed against this decision, but in 1996 his appeal was finally rejected by the highest Greek court. He subsequently complained to the Court in Strasbourg that he was treated as a person convicted of a felony when he applied for a professional post as a chartered accountant, despite the fact that the offence for which he had been convicted was prompted by his religious beliefs.

The Court upheld the applicant's complaint, finding there was a violation of Article 14 (prohibition of discrimination) in conjunction with Article 9 (freedom of thought, conscience and religion). His right not to be discriminated against in the enjoyment of the rights guaranteed under the Convention was violated when Greece, without an objective and reasonable justification, failed to treat differently persons whose situations were significantly different. The applicant's conviction did not imply dishonesty or turpitude likely to undermine his ability to exercise the profession of chartered accountant correctly. He was not an "unfit person" to exercise such a profession, as a common criminal would have been. There were no objective and reasonable grounds for not treating the applicant differently from other persons convicted of a felony (*Thlimmenos v. Greece, 2000*).

Another notable case claimed discrimination by the United Kingdom with regards to the different ages of retirement for men and women. The Court made use of its "margin of appreciation" and stated that the national authorities are better placed than the Court to appreciate the needs of their own society and therefore found the measures to be reasonable (*Stec and Others v. the United Kingdom, 2006*).

By the beginning of 2009, the Court had found violations of Article 14 in 123 cases, of which 33 involved the United Kingdom. Many of these were based on grounds of sex. In fact, the Court considers discrimination based on sex so important, that it may be presumed discriminatory. A number of women, who were legally resident in the UK, wanted their husbands to join them in the United Kingdom from abroad. The UK immigration authorities denied them permission, and the applicants successfully claimed discrimination, in conjunction with Article 8 (the right to family life).

They argued that, if they had wanted to join their husbands in the UK, permission would have been granted under UK law. The judges said, "Only very strong reasons could lead to a distinction based on sex being objectively justified" (*Abdulaziz, Cabales and Balkandali v. the United Kingdom, 1985*).

Another factor of discrimination that the ECHR proscribes explicitly is that of race. But the practice of "positive discrimination" – based on racial or other grounds – has yet to be tested before the Court and, as of now, there is no case law established on the matter.

In 2005, Protocol No. 12 of the ECHR entered into force, instituting a general prohibition of discrimination. The protection is extended to cover discrimination in the exercise of any legal right, even when that legal right is not explicitly protected under the Convention, so long as it is provided for in national law. To date, the protocol has been ratified by only 17 member states of the Council of Europe, and there are many notable absentee signatories, including France and the United Kingdom. Protocol No. 12 illustrates the Council of Europe's ongoing commitment to eradicate unjustifiable discrimination, but many member states, although prepared to sign the protocol, remain hesitant to ratify what appears to be such a broad qualification of their national legislation.

# The European Court of Human Rights

The ECHR not only set out a list of human rights to be protected, it also established the European Court of Human Rights. In its second section (Articles 19 to 51) the Convention lists the main purposes and procedures of the Court, which has then fleshed them out in more detail in its own Rules of Procedure.

The structure of the European Court of Human Rights was streamlined in 1998 to speed up its procedures and strengthen the right of individuals to submit their cases directly to the Court. Now new reforms are being introduced to reduce the backlog of cases pending.

Each of the 47 member states of the Council of Europe has the right to nominate candidates to become a judge at the Court. Candidates must be of high moral character and be legally qualified for high judicial office. Judges are elected for a six-year term of office by the Parliamentary Assembly of the Council of Europe from a short-list of three candidates put forward by each state. When appointed the chosen candidates sit in their individual capacity, not as servants of their state. They may not engage in any activity which is incompatible with their independence or impartiality. Judges may be re-elected to serve a further six years, but they must retire at age 70.

## One judge, three judges, seven or 17?

As in many legal systems, some of the procedures at the European Court of Human Rights are far from simple. The ECHR requires a certain procedure for litigants to bring applications to the Court, for decisions to be taken on whether they are admissible or not, and then how they are decided as to the substance of the issues at stake.

Facing long delays because of the rising number of applications, the member states negotiated a simplification of the original procedure in the form of an additional protocol (No. 14). For a long time, Russia delayed ratifying this protocol and the backlog of applications – many of them from Russia itself – continued to grow. Under some pressure from other member states, who isolated Russia by devising an alternative procedure to get round the delays for applications from their countries, the Russian authorities finally signalled that the Duma would indeed ratify the protocol, and so the revised procedures will now be put in place during 2010.

In summary, it is fair to say that the Court now works at four different levels. Applications are considered by just one judge to decide whether they are to be declared inadmissible. A committee of three judges considers the admissibility of applications which cannot be so simply declared inadmissible, and the three judges can go on to consider the merits of admissible cases that are the subject of well-established case law. A Chamber of seven judges considers cases that raise substantive issues or break new ground in the case law of the Court. And a Grand Chamber of 17 judges acts as the final level to which litigants or a Lower Chamber can ask to refer cases for consideration.

To be considered admissible, an application brought by an individual must have exhausted all domestic remedies in the home state concerned, and be lodged with the Court within six months of the end of that process. It may not be lodged anonymously, nor be substantially the same as a matter that the Court has already examined. Nor must it be manifestly ill-founded, or an abuse of the right of application.

## Backlog of cases, public proceedings, friendly settlement

The Court currently faces a tidal wave of applications rolling in at the rate of some 50 000 a year, and there is already a backlog of close to 100 000 applications. The Court regularly rejects many more applications than it

With 47 states in the Council of Europe, 800 million people have the right to apply to the Strasbourg Court if they feel their human rights have been infringed. In 1999 the Court received only 8 400 correctly completed applications. In 2009 this figure was over 50 000.

accepts, but it always gives reasons for declaring an application admissible or not. So great is the volume of applications, however, that delays are inevitable. It now takes on average well over two years for a case to work its way through the process of being accepted, heard and decided. The newly introduced procedure of one judge deciding on admissibility and a committee of three judges ruling on cases that relate to well established case law should help to reduce this time delay.

The procedure before the European Court of Human Rights is adversarial and public. But many cases are settled through a written procedure, simply on the basis of written evidence, and public hearings are held only in a minority of cases. Documents filed with the Court's registry by the parties are, in principle, open to the public. When the Court comes to its decision, it always gives the reasons for its judgment, and any dissenting judge may deliver a separate opinion.

Well over half the large number of pending applications are against just four member states: Russia (28%), Turkey (11%), Romania (9%) and Ukraine (8%).

In some cases the Court may seek a friendly settlement of the issue if it appears possible. Such proceedings are confidential, though subsequently they are confirmed with a decision briefly stating the facts and the solution reached.

## Chambers and the Grand Chamber

Having considered the written evidence and heard oral presentations by lawyers on both sides of the argument, a Chamber of seven judges gives a final judgment on cases that raise substantive issues or break new ground in the jurisprudence of the Court. But if one or other party in the case requests it, the case can be referred up to the Grand Chamber of

17 judges. A Chamber itself may also refer a case up to the Grand Chamber at any stage of the proceedings if the judges think that the implications of the issues concerned merit consideration by the highest authority within the Convention's procedure.

In nearly 40 years, between 1959 and 1998, the Court decided on just 837 cases. Since the reforms introduced in 1998, the Court has delivered over 10 000 judgments. The number of judgments given is currently about 1 500 per year. As a consequence, the resources of the Court have also expanded. In addition to the 47 judges, there are 270 lawyers working in Strasbourg in the Court's registry, supported by 370 secretarial and other support staff. The Court's annual budget is approximately 56 million euros and covers the judges' remuneration, staff salaries and operational expenditure such as IT, official travel, translation and interpretation, publications and legal aid.

> More than half the judgments delivered by the Court have concerned five of the member states: Italy and Turkey with roughly 2 000 judgments each, and France, Russia and Poland with approximately 700 each.

In recent years the Court has concentrated on examining complex cases, sometimes joining several applications together where they raise similar legal questions so that it can consider them jointly. Thus, although the number of judgments delivered each year is not rising as rapidly as in the past, the Court is examining more applications. With the recent reforms introduced in 2009, decisions on admissibility will be reached more quickly as well, and the backlog of cases should slowly be reduced.

## Follow through: executing judgments

The Court's judgments are binding on the member states concerned and have obliged individual governments to amend legislation and administrative practice in many fields. But it is the Committee of Ministers (representing all the states of the Council of Europe) that actually supervises the execution of judgments, not the Court itself.

The state concerned in any judgment reports periodically to the Committee on what steps it has taken to put right whatever it had done wrong, on

Election of the first Judges of the European Court of Human Rights in 1959.

compensation paid to litigants whose rights have been infringed, and what the state has done to remedy the situation for the future – such as changing a law or instructions given to public authorities in the exercise of their functions.

In 2009, for instance, the Committee met four times to supervise the execution of judgements, and at its last meeting of the year considered 374 new cases, some of which raised broader questions about how states would implement individual or general measures to obviate similar cases arising in the future. At the same meeting it also reviewed 500 legislative or other reforms that states have recently introduced, in 117 of which the necessary measures were now judged to be complete or almost complete.

The European Court of Human Rights has a keen interest in improving national procedures in order to reduce the flow of cases to Strasbourg. Ensuring human rights are respected better at home would lead to less litigation in Strasbourg. And in the last resort the Committee of Ministers can also draw public attention to a failure to execute Court judgments adequately by naming and shaming the state in question before the representatives of all the other states, in the hope that this will lead it to mend its ways. Not surprisingly, however, states are reluctant to do this for fear that one day the same treatment may be meted out to them.

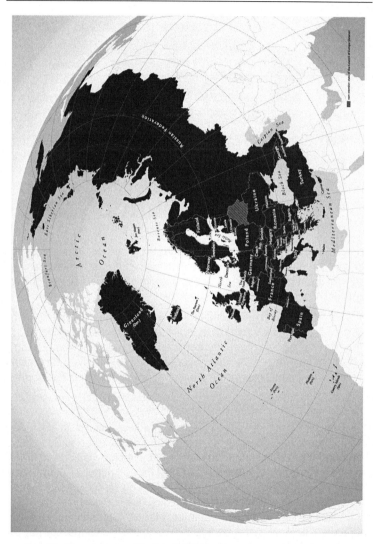

Map of the 47 member states of the Council of Europe.

# The broader picture of European human rights

The Convention and the European Court of Human Rights are the tip of the iceberg, the most immediately visible aspect of the broader system of human rights protection and promotion in the Council of Europe. They are vitally important, and they have been established longer than any other features of the system, but they do not stand alone. The member states of the Council of Europe are committed to the goals of democracy, human rights and the rule of law, and they have established several other bodies that contribute in different ways to promoting these goals.

## The Steering Committee for Human Rights (CDDH)

The Steering Committee for Human Rights co-ordinates the Council of Europe's multiple efforts to protect and promote human rights. Known by its French acronym, the CDDH (Comité Directeur des Droits de l'Homme), it is made up of representatives of the member states of the Council of Europe. Under the supervision of the Committee of Ministers, it oversees all the different strands of the Council of Europe's human rights activity – the Court, the Commissioner for Human Rights, the Parliamentary Assembly's Committee on Legal Affairs and Human Rights, the Commission for the Efficiency of Justice, the Committee for the Prevention of Torture, the Commission against Racism and Intolerance, and the Commission for Democracy through Law. The CDDH is charged in its terms of reference with the task of guaranteeing "coherence and synergies in the development of human rights law and policy".

The CDDH works through sub-committees of experts drawn from the member states. In 2009, groups of specialists met to discuss issues as varied as human rights and national minorities, human rights in the armed forces, non-discrimination, the issue of impunity and improving administrative procedures for the protection of human rights, in particular accelerated asylum procedures. It also keeps itself well informed about the work of other international groups working in related fields.

Recently the CDDH considered how to improve procedures at the European Court of Human Rights in order to reduce the backlog of applications and cases. It was in the CDDH – following up the 2007 Wise Persons Report on the effectiveness of the Court – that the latest series of procedural reforms (Protocol No. 14) were worked out. The CDDH is still working on further reforms – activating a network of government legal agents to consider pilot judgments and advisory opinions, encouraging states to associate themselves through "third party intervention" with cases not brought directly against themselves, and introducing new mechanisms for shortening the excessive time taken in some states for cases to come to trial.

## The European Commissioner for Human Rights

The post of European Commissioner for Human Rights was set up by the Council of Europe in 1997 – just a year after Russia joined the Council of Europe. Thomas Hammarberg, previously the Secretary General of Amnesty International, is the present Commissioner, and acts as an interlocutor for states to improve their observance of human rights. While the Commissioner cannot act on individual complaints, he can and does draw general conclusions and takes wider initiatives on the basis of information about human rights violations suffered by individuals. His overall task is to assist the Council of Europe in implementing its human rights standards.

He does this by conducting official missions to member states, ranging from a few days to a week or more, acting as a roving investigator in order to establish a comprehensive evaluation of the human rights situation there. He enjoys extensive contacts both with government and with non-government human rights organisations, and his reports, which are widely circulated and publicised, analyse the situation country by country. He opens a dialogue with governments about possible improvements, and his reports encourage practical reforms in order to achieve better human rights promotion and protection in the member states.

# The Parliamentary Committee on Legal Affairs and Human Rights

The Parliamentary Assembly of the Council of Europe (PACE) works through a committee of 84 parliamentarians to keep a political and legal eye on developments in the field of human rights. Its often outspoken reports lead to resolutions and recommendations addressed to member states and to other Council of Europe bodies.

The committee works through four sub-committees: human rights, criminal issues (including the fight against terrorism), the rights of minorities, and the election of judges to the Court. It also prepares the opinion of PACE on new conventions – recently, for example, on the Council of Europe Convention on Access to Official Documents. The committee focuses on four main strands of work: reinforcing the system of human rights protection in Europe, respecting human rights in the fight against terrorism, combating impunity, and combating discrimination.

At the committee's instigation, PACE recently urged member states to implement judgments of the Court more quickly, and to strengthen the authority and effectiveness of the ECHR. Through personal and party networks, MPs also played a useful role in talking to members of the Russian Duma, elucidating just why the Russian authorities were holding up the ratification of proposed reforms (Protocol No. 14) aimed at easing the European Court of Human Rights' workload and accelerating the delivery of judgments.

In 2006, a report by a member of the committee, Swiss Senator Dick Marty, exposed the scandal of CIA rendition flights and secret detention centres in Europe for terrorist suspects. PACE pressed member states to desist from any further complicity in the breach of fundamental human rights through aiding such practices. PACE also criticised black-listing individuals by the UN Security Council and the EU, as well as extending pre-charge detention for terrorist suspects as proposed by the UK Government.

PACE has criticised several states for their lack of co-operation in bringing perpetrators of serious crimes to justice. Whether it is the assassination of individual journalists or more widespread violations of human rights, for instance in Chechnya, debates in the committee and in PACE expose abuses and call for practical remedies. Reports have criticised the "blatant lack of political will" of some western Balkan states to prosecute war criminals. It has condemned disappearances as "on a par with torture and murder". Its current work includes reports on human rights violations in the North Caucasus, protecting human rights in emergency situations, "whistle blowers" and witness protection, and allegations of inhuman treatment of people and illicit trafficking of human organs in Kosovo.

# The European Committee for the Prevention of Torture (CPT)

The Council of Europe set up the European Committee for the Prevention of Torture and Inhuman or Degrading Treatment or Punishment in 1989 to do just that. The CPT visits places of detention in the member states – prisons, psychiatric hospitals, detention centres for aliens and juveniles, centres for the mentally disabled and the elderly – and inspects conditions there. In a given year it conducts 10 regular visits on a schedule planned well in advance and a further nine or 10 ad hoc visits at short notice.

The aim of the CPT is to combat torture and, by extension, any deliberate forms of ill-treatment. Following its visits it makes recommendations to the state concerned, suggesting improvements. These are discussed initially confidentially before a report on each visit is subsequently published. In almost all cases states co-operate closely with the CPT, not wishing to be named and shamed before their peers – and publicly – on what is a central issue of human rights. On only five occasions in the past 20 years has the CPT made a public statement when a state failed to co-operate or refused to improve the situation: Turkey in 1992 and 1996, and Russia in 2001, 2003 and most recently in 2007.

In the fight against terrorism since September 2001, states have been caught between their obligation to protect the safety of their citizens and their commitment to the ECHR, to uphold basic human rights. This tension manifests itself in various ways, such as extending the maximum periods of custody for terrorist suspects, limiting their access to a lawyer, or accepting diplomatic assurances from states with a poor human rights record when considering deportation of suspects. While there may be a case for adapting the existing legal framework, there is none for condoning illegal practices such as kidnapping by agents of the state, secret detention or "enhanced interrogation techniques". The CPT roundly declared: "Societies founded on human rights and the rule of law will not serve their interests well by jettisoning their basic values; on the contrary, it is in the defence of those values that lies ultimately their greatest security."

## The European Commission against Racism and Intolerance (ECRI)

The ECRI's remit is to combat racism, xenophobia, anti-Semitism and intolerance from the standpoint of the protection of human rights. The ECRI examines what states do to combat violence, discrimination and prejudice on grounds of race, colour, language, religion, nationality or national or ethnic origin. But it expressly excludes other forms of intolerance, such as homophobia, sexism or intolerance towards disabled people, since these are not part of its mandate. In an effort to protect and promote human rights, the ECRI's published reports, which are first discussed with the member state in question and then reviewed by all the others, often make uncomfortable reading.

The ECRI does not let any state off the hook by assuming all is well: it monitors all the Council of Europe member states on an equal footing, reviewing nine or 10 states each year over a five-year cycle. It is now into its fourth round of reviews, and in 2010, for instance, it will report on Albania, Austria, Estonia, France, Georgia, Poland, Serbia, the former Yugoslav Republic of Macedonia, Turkey and the United Kingdom. The ECRI also pursues follow-up visits two years after a report is published to see just what the member state has done about its conclusions.

For instance, the previous United Kingdom report surveyed, *inter alia*, recent legislation on citizenship, changes in the law on racially aggravated offences, incitement to racial hatred, the administration of legal aid, the reception and status of immigrants, asylum seekers and refugees, access to education and health services, particularly vulnerable groups such as Roma/ gypsies and travellers, Muslim and Jewish communities. It also reviewed the implementation of anti-terrorism legislation, and looked specifically at the effect of changes in asylum policies and the public perception of asylum seekers, refugees and minority groups.

# The European Commission for Democracy through Law (Venice Commission)

Human rights can be protected at a more fundamental level if the constitutional arrangements of a state reflect the basic values that promote individual human rights. That is what the European Commission for Democracy through Law is concerned with.

Over the 20 years since it was founded, in the city that gave it its name, the Venice Commission has evolved into an internationally respected independent legal think-tank, playing a role in crisis management and conflict prevention through constitution building and advice. And the advice it offers upholds the three essential principles of the Council of Europe: democracy, human rights and the rule of law. The Venice Commission advises states drafting basic laws so that they reflect the values of Europe's legal heritage.

From small beginnings, the work of the independent experts who make up the Venice Commission has proved so useful that now all 47 states of the Council of Europe are members, and states from outside Europe have joined as well: Kyrgyzstan, Chile, South Korea, Morocco, Algeria, Israel, Tunisia, Peru and Brazil. In addition, Argentina, Canada, the Holy See, Japan, Kazakhstan, Mexico, the United States and Uruguay co-operate closely with it as observers, as do international organisations such as the European Commission and the Organisation for Security and Co-operation in Europe (OSCE), all concerned and committed to ensuring that basic laws or constitutions encourage democracy, the rule of law and the protection of human rights.

# The European Commission for the Efficiency of Justice (CEPEJ)

A relatively recent creation, the CEPEJ was set up in 2002. It encourages member states to share a precise knowledge of their judicial systems so that they can identify weaknesses where justice is not well delivered and rights are poorly protected.

The CEPEJ carries out its task by preparing benchmarks against which to measure the delivery of different member states' judicial systems. It collects and analyses data, defines ways of evaluating judicial systems, adopts guidelines and action plans, promotes networks of legal professionals, NGOs, research institutes and information centres, and organises hearings. The CEPEJ is building a network where best practice can be encouraged through professional contact and exchanges, all with a view to promoting and protecting human rights better.

The CEPEJ has concentrated to date on issues such as the management of time by professionals in the judicial process, on the quality of justice and enforcement of judgments, and on alternatives to litigation – such as mediation. Sometimes the CEPEJ can help a member state meet the standards of the Council of Europe. In Malta and in Switzerland, for instance, it helped to advance mediation in civil, family and commercial matters. In Croatia and Slovenia it investigated ways of combating delays in the justice system, excessive workloads

> As the primary forum for the protection and promotion of human rights in Europe, the Council of Europe shall [ . . . ] play a dynamic role in protecting the right of individuals and promoting the invaluable engagement of non-government organisations, to actively defend human rights (Warsaw Action Plan, May 2005).

of judges and the backlog of cases. In Armenia it analysed the organisation of courts and encouraged reforms, and in the United Kingdom it assisted the government's strategy for restorative justice.

For the last five years the CEPEJ has sponsored a prize, the Crystal Scales of Justice, for innovative and efficient court practices. In 2009, for instance, prizes went to the Central Board Prison Service of Poland for their project on voluntary work by convicts in the local community, to the General Public Prosecutor's Office of Land Brandenburg for an electronic document management system, to the Czech Association for Probation and Mediation in Justice for a mentoring project, and to the Amsterdam District Court for a teaching project linking European criminal and human rights law: all examples of good practice that other states are encouraged to copy and learn from.

# What next for human rights?

As you can see from this description of the activities of various Council of Europe bodies, there is more to human rights than just the ECHR and the European Court of Human Rights. Taken together, all these organisations contribute to an incremental improvement in the protection and promotion of human rights across the continent and try to prevent any back-sliding by member states.

Now we shall consider a few ways in which human rights in Europe may develop over the coming years, from minor reforms in procedure to major shifts in focus. The closing pages of this short guide explore some of the questions raised by this expansion of human rights. Having charted where it has reached so far, we can point to where it might lead in the future.

## Expanding European human rights

"Human rights" is an umbrella term that covers a large body of law, essentially to do with the relationship between citizens and states. The Convention sets out the basic human rights that underpin this western democratic system: civil and political rights, including access to justice and the right to a fair trial.

Over the 60 years since the original Convention was agreed, the public authorities or governments of states have involved themselves in more and more social and economic activities. Contemporary governments have an enormous impact on how our societies function, engaging with citizens over a very broad range of issues, far more than when the ECHR was first drafted. Currently, for instance, governments take in taxes and spend on behalf of their citizens close to half the gross domestic product of most states in Europe. All of this activity is set within a framework of law and regulation, with rights and obligations for citizens as well as states.

The European statesmen who drew up the ECHR concentrated on political and civil rights in the original Convention, but from time to time revisions have widened the ECHR's scope to include – or at least imply – social and economic rights as well. Various protocols have been ratified, and other Council of Europe agreements – for instance, the European Social Charter – have been put in place to strengthen and enlarge the scope of human rights. This process has gradually elaborated a network of rights – social, economic, even environmental – which go beyond the hard core of civil and political rights in the original Convention. Different categories of beneficiaries have also been added, such as minorities, women and children, whose specific rights are to be ensured.

In the action plan they set up, following the summit meeting in Warsaw in 2005, the heads of government of the 47 member states of the Council of Europe put the "promotion of common fundamental values: human rights, rule of law and democracy" at the top of their list of priorities. And the first point they stressed was ensuring the continued effectiveness of the European Convention on Human Rights, improving the effectiveness of the European Court of Human Rights, followed by protection and promotion of human rights through the other Council of Europe institutions and mechanisms. They spelled out in particular steps they intended to take to strengthen the role of the Commissioner for Human Rights, the Committee for the Prevention of Torture (CPT) and the European Commission against Racism and Intolerance (ECRI).

## Improving the application of human rights law

Recently agreed reforms (Protocol No. 14) will doubtless help the Court to function better than it did before, in particular to weed out the applications which are not well enough founded to become cases. A lighter backlog of cases would then allow judges to spend more time on those which do raise substantive issues and require close attention and eventually judgment.

Beyond that, a better understanding of the ECHR by judges and the wider legal profession at national level would deliver better decisions nationally and help to stem the rising tide of applications to Strasbourg. More than

50% of pending applications come from just four countries – Russia 27%, Turkey 11%, Romania 9% and Ukraine 8% – so the Court is concerned to broaden the training of judges, in particular in these countries. A better understanding of European human rights, including the Court's own case law, should contribute to making the Court's work more effective and efficient by reducing the future flow of applications.

As part of this effort to improve the national application of European human rights law, the European Court of Human Rights has developed a procedure for "pilot judgments" over recent years to reduce the number of repetitive or similar cases that come to Court by encouraging member states to reform their legislation or administrative practice so that an effective remedy is offered nationally.

Encouraging member states to associate themselves with cases concerning other states might have a similar effect, since states take an interest in the judgments that affect them directly more than those which only involve other states. In that way, systemic problems – such as the length of national court proceedings – might be addressed jointly by several states, applying best practice across the board rather than responding in a piecemeal manner state by state. Similarly, efforts to strengthen the network of government agents directly responsible for monitoring the work of the European Court of Human Rights might help the exchange of information among them and stimulate a common understanding of the problems the Court faces and the solutions available to it.

During the Swiss presidency of the Committee of Ministers, the Court organised a conference in Switzerland on the 60th anniversary of the Convention. Ministers for foreign affairs and ministers of justice of the member states considered a number of possible improvements to the workings of the ECHR. They ranged from essentially small, practical suggestions for better using the existing Convention, to more radical changes which could imply "repatriating" some of the filtering work that accepts or rejects individual applications. The right of individual access to the Court could potentially be qualified by this, but it might also have the benefit of making national courts better aware of the nature and implications of European human rights law. After all, justice delivered well at national level is the ultimate goal of the ECHR.

# Social and other rights

The human rights that the ECHR guarantees are essentially civil and political rights. Social and economic rights lie beyond its scope, and these are safeguarded by the European Social Charter of the Council of Europe. Initially signed in 1961, this Charter was revised in 1996 both in the light of changing social expectations and of the extension of the number of states which had by then joined the Council of Europe. The revised Charter has been signed by all 47 of them, but ratified by only 29 of them to date, while 13 others have ratified the original Charter of 1961 but not yet ratified the revised version.

The Charter sets out a list of rights and freedoms relating to housing, health, education and employment, as well as certain aspects of legal and social protection (children and young offenders, prohibition of exploitation, protection of the family, the right to social security, welfare and services, protection from poverty and social exclusion, provision of childcare and measures to assist the elderly), aspects of free movement of persons (including family reunion and immigration formalities) and non-discrimination (including social integration of those with disabilities).

It also establishes a supervisory mechanism to guarantee respect of these rights by the states involved, setting up the European Committee of Social Rights. This consists of 15 independent and impartial individuals elected by the member states' representatives at the Council of Europe for a period of six years, renewable once. This committee reviews the national reports sent in by each state each year, describing how they implement the Charter both in law and in practice. The committee's conclusions are published and may criticise a state for not conforming to the Charter. If the state fails to change either the law or the practice criticised, member state representatives at the Council of Europe then step in to ask the state to rectify the situation.

Since some of the rights in the Charter relate to the concerns of NGOs as well as to major interest groups such as employers' federations or trade unions, a separate protocol permits collective complaints of violations to be submitted by NGOs – either those accredited to the Council of Europe or national ones – as well as by European and national unions and employers. To date, 14 member states have accepted this collective complaints procedure, but only Finland accepts the right of national NGOs to make use of it.

There is no right of individual recourse to the committee concerning the Social Charter. In this it is clearly different from the Court in respect of the ECHR, and this inevitably reduces the immediacy of its impact on the individual citizen. But it nonetheless serves a valuable purpose in buttressing the civil and political rights of the ECHR that are at the core of the Council of Europe's system of human rights protection with a secondary level of social and economic rights drawn up in a similar spirit. Member states are committed to both, even if the Social Charter is administered in a different fashion.

Contemporary debate around environmental issues such as climate change also refers to environmental rights, suggesting everybody has a right to clean air, fresh water and so on. While it is argued that such rights always enhance and in some cases are vital for a healthy existence, they also carry potentially heavy costs, and few states are yet prepared to offer guarantees for such rights, however desirable. But they may well be the next category of human rights that will enter serious discussion within the Council of Europe, particulary as the European Union, which is much more directly concerned with governmental policy on the environment and other economically sensitive issues, draws closer to the Council of Europe.

# Other beneficiaries:
## women, children, the disabled

Contemporary debate about human rights often goes beyond the general-ised aspiration of political and civil rights for everybody and envisages special rights for particular groups of people. In the European context these target children, women and those with disabilities. And in this, Europe reflects de-velopments at UN level, as it did 60 years ago when the ECHR was first drafted.

> The Council of Europe will, on the basis of its expertise and through its various organs, continue to provide support and advice to the European Union in particular in the fields of human rights and fundamental freedoms, democracy and the rule of law (Warsaw Action Plan, May 2005).

The UN Convention on the Elimination of All Forms of Discrimination against Women dates from 1979. In the same year, the Council of Europe began work on gender equality, and this developed 10 years later into a ministerial Declaration on Equality of Women and Men. At a subsequent ministerial meeting in Madrid in 2009, a further declaration was approved on "Making Gender Equality a Reality". The ministers who had previously agreed a recommendation on gender mainstreaming (in 1998), agreed a convention against trafficking in human beings (in 2005) and opened a campaign to combat violence against women (in 2006).

The UN Convention on the Rights of the Child dates from 1989, and the Parliamentary Assembly of the Council of Europe addressed a recommendation to the ministers of the member states in 1990 to consider children's rights. In 1996 the member states agreed a European Convention on the Exercise of Children's Rights, ensuring that children gained procedural rights in judicial proceedings before family courts. More recently, the Council of Europe has also opened an awareness-raising campaign aimed at the general public to prevent corporal punishment for children.

The UN Convention on the Rights of Persons with Disabilities dates from 2007, and it would be fair to say that the Council of Europe was ahead of the game by declaring 2003 the European Year of People with Disabilities. In 2006 ministers agreed an action plan to promote the rights and full participation of people with disabilities in society. The action plan runs until 2015 and concentrates on the right to work, the right to access, to education, to make choices in life and to participate. In implementing the action plan member states are encouraged to pay special attention to specific groups such as women and girls, children and young people, ageing people, people from minorities and migrants with disabilities.

# EU accession to the ECHR

The European Court of Human Rights in Strasbourg is sometimes confused with the European Court of Justice in Luxembourg. The names may be similar, but their functions are very different. The former has formed the major subject of this book, the Court which interprets the European Convention of Human Rights or ECHR. The latter is the Court of the European Union, concerned essentially with economic and administrative issues. As Terry Davis, the former Secretary General of the Council of Europe, succinctly put it: "The Council of Europe deals with the quality of life, while the European Union deals with the standard of living."

Over time, the two organisations have developed separate legal structures and jurisdictions which lead to confusion in the popular mind. While all 27 member states of the EU are also members of the Council of Europe and subscribe to the ECHR, the EU itself does not. Now with the ratification of the Lisbon Treaty it has been given the legal authority to do so, and – assuming no opposition from other members of the Council of Europe – is likely to do so in the near future.

What is the point? What advantages will that bring for the protection and promotion of human rights?

When the EU does subscribe to the ECHR, it will submit the EU's legal system to independent external control by the Court in Strasbourg, giving European citizens the same protection vis-à-vis acts of the EU itself as they already enjoy vis-à-vis acts of their member states.

Fortunately, the judges at both the European Court of Justice in Luxembourg and the European Court of Human Rights in Strasbourg have been well aware of the possible conflict of jurisdictions. They have taken care to keep their judgments broadly in alignment with each other's principles over recent years. The European Court of Justice often cites the case law of the European Court of Human Rights in its judgments, and the European Court of Human Rights already takes note of decisions from the European Court of Justice wherever relevant. Bringing the two into a formal legal relationship does not appear problematic in practice. But the EU signing the ECHR is likely to bring with it an additional judge from the EU to join the 47 from the member states of the Council of Europe at the Strasbourg Court, and – through a modification of the statute which currently only allows states to join – the accession of the EU to the Council of Europe itself. That opens a much bigger question of the relations between the two organisations.

The EU could well then sign and ratify many of the conventions of the Council of Europe and transpose into EU-wide legislation the standards of the Council of Europe as reflected in its conventions. It may all seem a little arcane, but the end result will be a more comprehensive protection of human rights across Europe, strengthening the field of application of the ECHR and the role of the European Court of Human Rights. As the current Secretary General of the Council of Europe, Thorbjørn Jagland, put it when the Treaty of Lisbon finally came into effect towards the end of 2009, "This will be good for human rights and good for Europe". The final declaration of the meeting of the heads of government of all 47 members states of the Council of Europe in Warsaw in 2005 expressed it in somewhat more bureaucratic language:

> Enhanced partnership and complementarity should govern the future relationship between the Council of Europe and the European Union, in order to strengthen practical co-operation in all areas of common interest.

That should benefit everyone in Europe.

# References

## Websites

Human rights bodies

Council of Europe: www.coe.int

European Court of Human Rights' case law portal: www.echr.coe.int/ECHR/EN/Header/Case-Law/HUDOC/HUDOC+database

Amnesty International: www.amnesty.org

Human Rights First: www.humanrightsfirst.org

Human Rights Watch: www.hrw.org

Liberty: www.liberty-human-rights.org.uk

## Human rights texts

The Universal Declaration of Human Rights: www.un.org/en/documents/udhr

European Convention of Human Rights: www.conventions.coe.int/treaty/EN/Treaties/html/005.htm

## Human rights courts

European Court of Human Rights: www.echr.coe.int

African Court on Human and Peoples' Rights: www.african-court.org

Inter-American Court of Human Rights: www.corteidh.or.cr

## Books

Donnelly J. (2003), *Universal Human Rights in Theory and Practice* (2nd edn), Cornell University Press, USA.

Foster S. (2008), *Human Rights and Civil Liberties* (2nd edn), Pearson, UK.

Gomien D. (2005), *Short Guide to the European Convention on Human Rights*, Council of Europe Publishing, Strasbourg.

Hollo L. Y. (2009), *The European Commission against Racism and Intolerance (ECRI) – its first 15 years*, Council of Europe Publishing, Strasbourg.

McBride J. (2009), *Human rights and criminal procedure – The case law of the European Court of Human Rights*, Council of Europe Publishing, Strasbourg.

Morgan R. and Evans M. (2001), *Combating torture in Europe – The work and standards of the European Committee for the Prevention of Torture*, Council of Europe Publishing, Strasbourg.

Renucci J. F. (2005), *Introduction to the European Convention on Human Rights – The rights guaranteed and the protection mechanism*, Council of Europe Publishing, Strasbourg.

## Sales agents for publications of the Council of Europe
## Agents de vente des publications du Conseil de l'Europe

**BELGIUM/BELGIQUE**
La Librairie Européenne -
The European Bookshop
Rue de l'Orme, 1
BE-1040 BRUXELLES
Tel.: +32 (0)2 231 04 35
Fax: +32 (0)2 735 08 60
E-mail: order@libeurop.be
http://www.libeurop.be

Jean De Lannoy/DL Services
Avenue du Roi 202 Koningslaan
BE-1190 BRUXELLES
Tel.: +32 (0)2 538 43 08
Fax: +32 (0)2 538 08 41
E-mail: jean.de.lannoy@dl-servi.com
http://www.jean-de-lannoy.be

**BOSNIA AND HERZEGOVINA/
BOSNIE-HERZÉGOVINE**
Robert's Plus d.o.o.
Marka Maruliça 2/V
BA-71000, SARAJEVO
Tel.: + 387 33 640 818
Fax: + 387 33 640 818
E-mail: robertsplus@bih.net.ba

**CANADA**
Renouf Publishing Co. Ltd.
1-5369 Canotek Road
CA-OTTAWA, Ontario K1J 9J3
Tel.: +1 613 745 2665
Fax: +1 613 745 7660
Toll-Free Tel.: (866) 767-6766
E-mail: order.dept@renoufbooks.com
http://www.renoufbooks.com

**CROATIA/CROATIE**
Robert's Plus d.o.o.
Marasoviçeva 67
HR-21000, SPLIT
Tel.: + 385 21 315 800, 801, 802, 803
Fax: + 385 21 315 804
E-mail: robertsplus@robertsplus.hr

**CZECH REPUBLIC/
RÉPUBLIQUE TCHÈQUE**
Suweco CZ, s.r.o.
Klecakova 347
CZ-180 21 PRAHA 9
Tel.: +420 2 424 59 204
Fax: +420 2 848 21 646
E-mail: import@suweco.cz
http://www.suweco.cz

**DENMARK/DANEMARK**
GAD
Vimmelskaftet 32
DK-1161 KØBENHAVN K
Tel.: +45 77 66 60 00
Fax: +45 77 66 60 01
E-mail: gad@gad.dk
http://www.gad.dk

**FINLAND/FINLANDE**
Akateeminen Kirjakauppa
PO Box 128
Keskuskatu 1
FI-00100 HELSINKI
Tel.: +358 (0)9 121 4430
Fax: +358 (0)9 121 4242
E-mail: akatilaus@akateeminen.com
http://www.akateeminen.com

**FRANCE**
La Documentation française
(diffusion/distribution France entière)
124, rue Henri Barbusse
FR-93308 AUBERVILLIERS CEDEX
Tél.: +33 (0)1 40 15 70 00
Fax: +33 (0)1 40 15 68 00
E-mail: commande@ladocumentationfrancaise.fr
http://www.ladocumentationfrancaise.fr

Librairie Kléber
1 rue des Francs Bourgeois
FR-67000 STRASBOURG
Tel.: +33 (0)3 88 15 78 88
Fax: +33 (0)3 88 15 78 80
E-mail: librairie-kleber@coe.int
http://www.librairie-kleber.com

**GERMANY/ALLEMAGNE
AUSTRIA/AUTRICHE**
UNO Verlag GmbH
August-Bebel-Allee 6
DE-53175 BONN
Tel.: +49 (0)228 94 90 20
Fax: +49 (0)228 94 90 222
E-mail: bestellung@uno-verlag.de
http://www.uno-verlag.de

**GREECE/GRÈCE**
Librairie Kauffmann s.a.
Stadiou 28
GR-105 64 ATHINAI
Tel.: +30 210 32 55 321
Fax.: +30 210 32 30 320
E-mail: ord@otenet.gr
http://www.kauffmann.gr

**HUNGARY/HONGRIE**
Euro Info Service
Pannónia u. 58.
PF. 1039
HU-1136 BUDAPEST
Tel.: +36 1 329 2170
Fax: +36 1 349 2053
E-mail: euroinfo@euroinfo.hu
http://www.euroinfo.hu

**ITALY/ITALIE**
Licosa SpA
Via Duca di Calabria, 1/1
IT-50125 FIRENZE
Tel.: +39 0556 483215
Fax: +39 0556 41257
E-mail: licosa@licosa.com
http://www.licosa.com

**MEXICO/MEXIQUE**
Mundi-Prensa México, S.A. De C.V.
Río Pánuco, 141 Delegacion Cuauhtémoc
MX-06500 MÉXICO, D.F.
Tel.: +52 (01)55 55 33 56 58
Fax: +52 (01)55 55 14 67 99
E-mail: mundiprensa@mundiprensa.com.mx
http://www.mundiprensa.com.mx

**NETHERLANDS/PAYS-BAS**
Roodveldt Import BV
Nieuwe Hemweg 50
NE-1013 CX AMSTERDAM
Tel.: + 31 20 622 8035
Fax.: + 31 20 625 5493
Website: www.publidis.org
E-mail: orders@publidis.org

**NORWAY/NORVÈGE**
Akademika
Postboks 84 Blindern
NO-0314 OSLO
Tel.: +47 2 218 8100
Fax: +47 2 218 8103
E-mail: support@akademika.no
http://www.akademika.no

**POLAND/POLOGNE**
Ars Polona JSC
25 Obroncow Street
PL-03-933 WARSZAWA
Tel.: +48 (0)22 509 86 00
Fax: +48 (0)22 509 86 10
E-mail: arspolona@arspolona.com.pl
http://www.arspolona.com.pl

**PORTUGAL**
Livraria Portugal
(Dias & Andrade, Lda.)
Rua do Carmo, 70
PT-1200-094 LISBOA
Tel.: +351 21 347 42 82 / 85
Fax: +351 21 347 02 64
E-mail: info@livrariaportugal.pt
http://www.livrariaportugal.pt

**RUSSIAN FEDERATION/
FÉDÉRATION DE RUSSIE**
Ves Mir
17b, Butlerova ul.
RU-101000 MOSCOW
Tel.: +7 495 739 0971
Fax: +7 495 739 0971
E-mail: orders@vesmirbooks.ru
http://www.vesmirbooks.ru

**SPAIN/ESPAGNE**
Mundi-Prensa Libros, s.a.
Castelló, 37
ES-28001 MADRID
Tel.: +34 914 36 37 00
Fax: +34 915 75 39 98
E-mail: libreria@mundiprensa.es
http://www.mundiprensa.com

**SWITZERLAND/SUISSE**
Planetis Sàrl
16 chemin des pins
CH-1273 ARZIER
Tel.: +41 22 366 51 77
Fax: +41 22 366 51 78
E-mail: info@planetis.ch

**UNITED KINGDOM/ROYAUME-UNI**
The Stationery Office Ltd
PO Box 29
GB-NORWICH NR3 1GN
Tel.: +44 (0)870 600 5522
Fax: +44 (0)870 600 5533
E-mail: book.enquiries@tso.co.uk
http://www.tsoshop.co.uk

**UNITED STATES and CANADA/
ÉTATS-UNIS et CANADA**
Manhattan Publishing Company
468 Albany Post Road
US-CROTON-ON-HUDSON, NY 10520
Tel.: +1 914 271 5194
Fax: +1 914 271 5856
E-mail: Info@manhattanpublishing.com
http://www.manhattanpublishing.com

**Council of Europe Publishing/Éditions du Conseil de l'Europe**
FR-67075 STRASBOURG Cedex
Tel.: +33 (0)3 88 41 25 81 – Fax: +33 (0)3 88 41 39 10 – E-mail: publishing@coe.int – Website: http://book.coe.int